SOLVED!

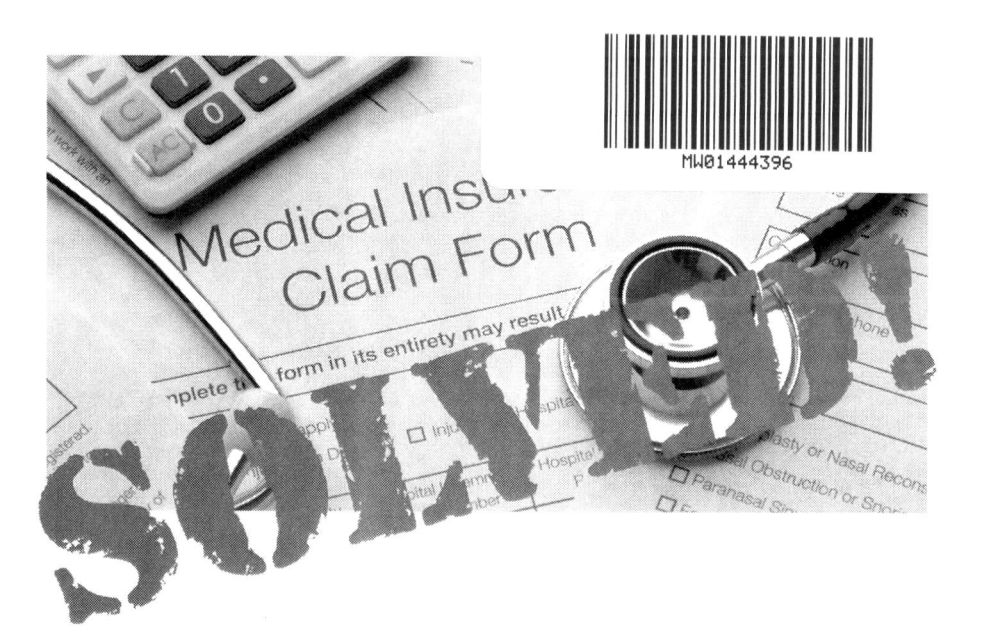

Curing Your Medical Insurance Problems

ADVICE FROM MedWise INSURANCE ADVOCACY

Adria Goldman Gross, FIPC
Douglas Winslow Cooper, Ph.D.

"Learn what to watch out for......" Ralph Nader

USA EDITION OF – *Multi-Payer Medicine Nightmare MADE IN THE USA*

Cover Design By - Gilbert Design Inc.

outskirtspress
DENVER, COLORADO

The opinions expressed in this manuscript are solely the opinions of the author and do not represent the opinions or thoughts of the publisher. The author has represented and warranted full ownership and/or legal right to publish all the materials in this book.

Solved! Curing Your Medical Insurance Problems
Advice from MedWise Insurance Advocacy
All Rights Reserved.
Copyright © 2015 Adria Goldman Gross, FIPC and Douglas Winslow Cooper, Ph.D.
v2.0

Cover Image by Mitch Gilbert
Author photo [AGG] by clicksbykaren.com
Author photo [DWC] by Jeremy Landolfa

This book may not be reproduced, transmitted, or stored in whole or in part by any means, including graphic, electronic, or mechanical without the express written consent of the publisher except in the case of brief quotations embodied in critical articles and reviews.

Outskirts Press, Inc.
http://www.outskirtspress.com

ISBN: 978-1-4787-6056-6

Outskirts Press and the "OP" logo are trademarks belonging to Outskirts Press, Inc.

PRINTED IN THE UNITED STATES OF AMERICA

Dedication

We thank our families, mentors, and friends. You have supported, guided, educated, and uplifted us, and we hope to return some of those benefits to others through our book.

Adria Goldman Gross, FIPC   Douglas Winslow Cooper, Ph.D.

Table of Contents

Acknowledgments i

Preface to the American Edition iii

Foreword v

Introduction: Are You "Fee-Wise" about Medical Bills and Insurance Coverage? vii
    The Problem vii
    The Solution vii
    Who Are the Authors? viii
    What Will You Learn? xi
    We Promise xii
    Your Opportunity and Responsibility xii

1:   Leaving My Seizures Behind 1

2:   Patient Becomes Patient Advocate 11

3:   Diagnosing and Reducing Your Medical Bills 15
    How to Cut Your Medical Bills 15
    Is This Test Required? Why Is This Test Required? Save Money! 16
    Options for the Uninsured and Underinsured 17
    Medical Tourism 18
    Drugs from Canada 20
    Drugs from Mexico 20

Don't Assume Your Bill Is Correct / How Medical Bills Came into Being 21
Tiered Payments 21
Health Insurance Portability and Accountability Act of 1996: Privacy 22
One Visit – Ten Bills – WHY? 22
Who Is Processing Your Medical Bill? 23
How to Decode the Bill? 24
What to Do with the Bill Once Decoded? Is the Bill within Reasonable
    and Customary Charges? 24
Appropriate Usage for GY Code 24
Inappropriate Usage for GY Code 24
Taking Action in Order to Decrease Your Bill 25
The Buck Stops Here 26
Tying It All Together 26
Catching the Errors 26

4:   Hospital Over-Charges 28
    Ask These Five Questions about Medical Expenses to Avoid Over-Paying 28

5:   Successful Challenges 31
    Patient Beware—and Be Informed! 31
    Confronting the Admissions Confusion 32
    Insurance Advocacy Saved a Client $98,000 in Medical Expenses 33
    A Nursing Home's Collections Case Became a Big Refund for the Client Instead ... 33
    Advocating for Access to Information the Health Facility Denied the Patient 34
    Explore How Initial Claim Was Prepared and Filed, Understand
        What Is Covered in Your Health Plans 34
    A Medical Insurance Advocate Can Help You Recoup Money You Are Owed,
        and Keep You from Paying What You Don't Owe 37
    What a Medical Insurance Advocate Does 38
    Before You Pay Those Medical Bills 39
    Hire a Medical Insurance Advocate? Eight Good Reasons Why You Should 40
    Turning Ten Denials into More Than $40,000 40
    Fight Insurance Companies and Medical Providers on Contested Charges,
        Confusing Bills 41
    Medical Insurance Advocacy Cases 42

6: Medicare Considerations 44
   Avoid the Intense Pain When "Admitted to Hospital" Is Not What You Think 44
   Coverage for Inpatient or Outpatient Procedures 45
   What You Can Do 47

7: Medicare Appeals Information 48
   Medicare.gov, "The Official U.S. Government Site for Medicare" 48
   Official U.S. Government Medicare Handbook, Medicare & You. 49
   If You Have Original Medicare 50
   If You Have a Medicare Health Plan 50
   If You Have a Medicare Prescription Drug Plan 50
   Advanced Beneficiary Notice of Noncoverage (ABN) 51

8: Affordable Care Act ["Obama Care"] Appeals 52
   Appealing Health Plan Decisions 52
   Internal Appeals 53
   External Review 53
   What This Means for You 53
   Some Important Details 54
   For More Information 54

9: Out-of-Network Protection Legislation 55
   What's a Surprise Bill? 56
   New Disclosures Help Avoid Financial Distress 57

10: Medicare Supplement (Medigap) Plans 60
    Compare Medigap Plans Side-by-Side 60
    United Healthcare Medigap Appeals and Grievances Process 62
    Member Grievances 63

11: Medicare Advantage Plans 64

12: Catastrophic Coverage Plans 67
    Protection from Worst-case Scenarios 67
    Catastrophic Plans with a Hardship Exemption 68
    The Hardship Exemptions 68

13: Patient Information Resources 70

Appendix 1: About MedWise Insurance Advocacy 79
Appendix 2: Award Nominations for Adria Goldman Gross 85
Appendix 3: Testimonials for MedWise and Adria Goldman Gross 93

Acknowledgments

A book not only has parents, it has aunts and uncles, and even the occasional cousin, all of whom help make it what it becomes. We happily and warmly thank the professionals in our creative "family" who helped us bring this book to fruition:

Bill Bauer, Sherry Korner, Iris Sandow, and Bob Tarr gave their skilled, friendly assistance by commenting on early drafts.

Dr. Carmen McBean Becker has served as Adria's mentor and inspiring friend. A woman with an amazing life history, she herself is in the midst of book authorship.

Cheryl C. Cohen provided editorial assistance in the book's final stages, shortly before its birth.

Jay and Louise Dankberg gave us valuable advice on how to call the book to the attention of those likely to benefit from it.

Mitch Gilbert, Adria Gross's cousin, designed our cover and helped create the title, two elements known to influence the likelihood that someone will give the book a chance to help them.

Edison Guzman has coached both of us, and if not for his help, we would not be where we are now.

Robin Fischer Hoerber has been Adria's mentor and her inspirational friend since Adria was 12 years old; Robin has been blind since birth but has not let that stop her.

Bill Hogan we have been honored to have as a friend and guide.

Harley Matsil's way with words helped name both the book and, earlier, the MedWise business.

Laurie Salkin, Adria's supportive, successful, beautiful "little sister," a dear friend for over 16 years.

Karen Schustermann Pomerantz and **Julia Simons:** we give thanks for proofreading by these two of Adria's Monroe friends, whom she met around 1997.

Caryn Starr-Gates, writer and friend, crafted significant portions of the original material from which this book was ultimately derived.

Robin Yarrington contributed her valuable editorial help as the book was nearing completion.

Preface to the American Edition

I [AGG] **had to write this book**. My decades of experience with medical practice billing and insurance claim handling rudely educated me about the high frequency of erroneous billing and mistaken denial of medical insurance coverage claims.

Problems with medical bills can cause a tremendous bankruptcy. If we had a system like "single-payer" [government-only], I would be out of business.

I saw how hard life could be for those whose medical conditions left them weak, confused, and sometimes impoverished, lacking the information and expertise that would help them uncover and correct unfair medical charges and inappropriate denials of their insurance claims.

Keep from being cheated by medical practitioners or organizations who would over-charge you, deliberately or inadvertently, and prevent your being short-changed by those insurers who would under-compensate you for your legitimate medical expenditures.

Even the excessively slow payment of justifiable expenses can bankrupt patients who had no idea their medical care would be so costly or who thought they were covered by insurance, only to find that one or more of their doctors was "out of network," making the patients "out of luck" and having to pay the full, sometimes exorbitant, medical bills. Knowing how the system works can help you speed up the process.

Baffling billing by hospitals and doctors combined with obscure exceptions, conditions, or requirements in their medical insurance policies leave many people feeling overwhelmed just when at their weakest.

I became determined to write and speak on behalf of the mistreated and the bilked, using the expertise I had obtained in my decades in the medical billing and insurance fields.

I hope our book will bring valuable resources and needed reassurance to those caught in our modern medical money maelstrom.

Adria Goldman Gross, FIPC, MedWise Insurance Advocacy
adria@MedWisebilling.com

Having fought successfully to win millions of dollars of continuing medical insurance coverage for my wife, bedridden with multiple sclerosis for over two decades, with around-the-clock skilled nursing for the past eleven years, I [DWC] was pleased to assist patient advocate Adria Goldman Gross in preparing this book to help others succeed in catching medical billing errors and obtaining the private insurance and government support they deserve for medical care for themselves and their loved ones.

Douglas Winslow Cooper, Ph.D.
douglas@tingandi.com

Foreword

They survived two Supreme Court challenges, and with the third open-enrollment season now fast approaching, many are wondering what the "next story" is for the exchanges created under the Affordable Care Act. We've all seen the headlines: the rise of so-called narrow networks, the increase in high-deductible consumer-driven plans, and the "sticker-shock" patients face with unexpectedly high medical bills.

But what does this all mean for patients? In this book, Adria Goldman Gross and Douglas Winslow Cooper arm patients with the knowledge they need to navigate the financial side of the U.S. medical system. Through personal reflection and in-depth analysis, the authors share detailed tips on how readers can spot over-charges by their doctors or hospitals, under-payments by their health plans, and incorrect denials by their insurance.

Ms. Gross brings to bear years of experience as an insurance insider to her work as an independent patient advocate to help her clients reduce their medical bills. Much of what Ms. Gross does for her clients, patients can do for themselves with the help of this book. This is a must-read for anyone who's felt lost, angry, or confused after receiving a medical bill.

Andrew Fitch, Product Manager at NerdWallet

Introduction: Are You "Fee-Wise" about Medical Bills and Insurance Coverage?

The Problem
According to studies, 80% of medical bills contain fees that are incorrect, often inflated to favor the practitioner. Corresponding insurance claims are often processed in a manner that is incorrect or underpays a covered service. Individual patients are often unaware of billing and insurance errors. Furthermore, consumers are often frustrated by their lack of effective mechanisms to resolve an overcharge. You want to spot such errors, contest them, and get them corrected.

The Solution
Individuals can protect themselves against billing and insurance coverage errors. To do so, you need to understand your medical bills and your insurance coverage. The insights and the steps described here will help you keep from being taken advantage of. In some cases, you will be able to spot the errors yourself, contact the institution, and obtain correction.

As one of us, Douglas Winslow Cooper, did, you may have to pursue a lengthy appeal process on your own to get your insurance company to pay the bills.

In other cases, you may require professional assistance from a medical insurance advocate, like Adria Goldman Gross, President and founder of MedWise Insurance Advocacy. You will learn here about the following examples of successful appeals handled by MedWise:

1. Denied claim on an in-state procedure overturned,
2. Getting coverage for an out-of-state emergency surgery,
3. A vacation accident that led to international disputes between foreign hospitals and the domestic insurer,
4. An over-charged lab bill was reduced from $9,000 to less than $400.
5. Insurance case was closed by getting physician's bills aligned with customary, allowable charges.
6. Proving the client had no additional insurance and needed emergency hospitalization yielded payment in full for hospital charges.

This book will help you find the errors, correct them, contest them, and appeal an unfavorable decision, if necessary. It will give you added confidence to fight and win.

Who Are the Authors?

Adria Goldman Gross, founder and President of MedWise Insurance Advocacy, based in Monroe, New York, has achieved extraordinary results for her clients by working out highly beneficial arrangements for those who have exhausted all other options. Since founding her practice in January 2012, she has recovered for her clients over $1,000,000 per year in medical expenses that insurers tried to block or that healthcare providers erroneously charged.

Adria became involved in advocacy after her own experience with the medical system, as described in this book's first chapter, "Leaving My Seizures Behind."

Adria is a New York State-licensed insurance broker and

consultant, and a certified medical billing and medical claims expert—she contacts appropriate state financial and legal agencies, such as CMS Medicare/Medicaid, health care providers, and insurance companies, to help ensure patient rights and to see that her clients get the coverage for which they are paying. She stresses that diligence and perseverance are frequently required and that cases often must go to the state insurance authorities for resolution.

As a medical insurance advocate, Adria is the liaison between patient or attorney, insurance company, and medical provider to work out a solution that resolves billing disputes.

The acronym FIPC after Adria Goldman Gross's name stands for "Federation of Insurance Professionals Certification." Adria is a member, writes articles, speaks at, and attends classes through:

- Insurance Professionals of Orange County
- ACAP - Alliance of Claims Assistance Professionals
- NAHAC - National Association of Healthcare Advocacy Consultants
- APHA - The Alliance of Professional Health Advocates
- AAPC - American Academy of Professional Coders
- AMBA - American Medical Billing Association
- PPAI - Professional Patient Advocate Institute
- NerdWallet

CONTACT INFORMATION:
Adria Goldman Gross
MedWise Insurance Advocacy, Division of MedWise Billing, Inc.
24 Pawtuxet Avenue
Monroe, NY 10950
845-238-2532
adria@MedWisebilling.com

SEE ALSO:
>http://www.adriagross.com
>http://www.medicalinsuranceadvocacy.com
>http://www.facebook.com/MedWiseInsuranceAdvocacy
>http://www.MedWisebilling.com/
>http://www.facebook.com/MedWiseBillingInc

Douglas Winslow Cooper, Ph.D., is a writer, editor, and retired environmental scientist, who for over a decade has helped to manage continuous, at-home, skilled nursing care for his wife, Tina Su Cooper, who is quadriplegic and ventilator-dependent due to multiple sclerosis.

Dr. Cooper's experience with medical billing and insurance coverage has come primarily from handling issues associated with the extensive medical care needed by his wife. As described later, he successfully appealed originally adverse insurance decisions concerning paying for the skilled nursing care of his wife at home, appeals that preserved insurance payments of approximately $400,000 per year in coverage for her care, now totaling approximately $4 million.

Douglas earned his A.B., with honors, in physics at Cornell, served at the U.S. Army biological warfare laboratories at Ft. Detrick, MD, returned to school, and obtained his M.S. degree in physics at Penn State, and then his Ph.D. in engineering from Harvard. His professional life centered on environmental issues.

He served as an Associate Professor at the Harvard Graduate School of Public Health and subsequently as a Research Staff Member at IBM's Yorktown Heights, NY, Thomas J. Watson, Jr., Research Center.

Dr. Cooper was the author or co-author of more than 100 technical articles published in refereed journals and was elected Fellow of the Institute of Environmental Sciences. He now does freelance writing, book coaching, partnering, and editing. He wrote *Ting and I: A Memoir of Love, Courage, and Devotion,* co-authored three other memoirs, and edited three other non-fiction books.

CONTACT INFORMATION:
Douglas Winslow Cooper, Ph.D.
264 East Drive, Walden, NY 12586
douglas@tingandi.com
http://writeyourbookwithme.com

What Will You Learn?

- You'll find 10 ways to prepare, before you are admitted to a hospital, to reduce your medical bills.
- You'll learn the Medicare rules for Inpatient and Outpatient status, which can significantly affect billing and re-imbursement.
- You'll be made alert to the crucial distinction for insurance coverage between "in-network" and "out-of-network" medical providers.
- You'll find what to look for in hospital bills to catch errors and prevent over-charging.
- Before you go overseas for "medical tourism," read about insurance coverage issues here.
- Before you order prescription drugs from Canada or Mexico, note our comments.
- Is that trip in an ambulance covered? Depends on your policy's terms; e.g., whether a stretcher was needed.
- What are CPTs? What is ICD-10 and where can you get detailed information about it?
- Why does one hospitalization produce a dozen or so bills?
- You'll learn common causes of medical billing errors and what to do about them.
- What charges are "reasonable and customary," and why does it matter?
- You'll become aware of the dreaded GY Codes that mean "insurance company, do not pay this."
- You'll see examples of successful challenges and negotiations

to reduce bills and increase insurance pay-outs. So, don't assume your bills are correct. Inspect them. Challenge them. Pay less.

You will become familiar with the services of medical insurance advocates for situations beyond your ability to handle. For example in a couple of recent cases, MedWise saved a family $220,000 in medical expenses that originally totaled $227,000 and won a $43,000 judgment for a New York man whose appeals had been denied ten times by his insurer. Recently, MedWise, within a two-week period, saved two separate patients over $500,000 in over-charges on medical bills.

We Promise

You will become a more well-informed consumer of medical services, better prepared to examine your bills, spot errors, and get them corrected, often at substantial financial savings.

Your Opportunity and Responsibility

Although this book can be used as a reference, we recommend you read it through as soon as possible, so you are already prepared before you find yourself sick, tired, confused, and over-charged or under-covered.

1
Leaving My Seizures Behind

The jewelry department of Lord & Taylor's on Fifth Avenue in Manhattan is a rather embarrassing place to be arrested, but I [AGG] could not utter a word of protest to the burly New York cop who was twisting my arms behind my back to handcuff me. A crowd had gathered to gawk at me in the aisle where I had fallen, and the cops had roped me off while I was unconscious.

Now, as my consciousness returned after the grand mal epileptic seizure, I wanted desperately just to leave, to flee Lord & Taylor's for the anonymity of the streets of Midtown Manhattan. But I could not speak, could not understand why they were preventing me from leaving, could not comprehend why they would take me, hands cuffed behind my back, like a thief caught taking one of the watches I had come there to purchase. They forcibly took me to their squad car waiting at the store's entrance and ferried me to a hospital.

This was just the latest in a series of embarrassing experiences prompted by years of grand mal seizures, and by the time my speech capacities returned a couple of hours later, I was in the hospital emergency room, crying my eyes out.

"Please," I pleaded with the emergency room personnel, "I just had a grand mal. I was in Lord & Taylor's when it happened. I couldn't speak. I want to leave and the police handcuffed me. Please take the handcuffs off and let me go." I had to repeat myself several times, but when they finally understood my situation, the emergency room people told the cops to take the handcuffs off.

They let me go. Profoundly shaken, I took the subway home.

In the twenty-three years (my ages 12 to 35) of my affliction with post-encephalitis epilepsy, I had come to experience a wide range of emotions and situations, many of them fraught with tremendous personal embarrassment, discomfort, and outright pain. Even though the worst of the seizures created many intensely embarrassing--and some life-threatening--moments for me, the lessons in caring that I learned from growing up with epilepsy will remain with me long after the pain I had to endure learning those lessons has vanished.

Only when I had reached a point of absolute desperation, after my first marriage, my career, and my self-confidence had been completely shattered, did I discover the miracle that was able to resurrect the joy and pleasure in living that I had known as a girl growing up in Port Jervis, New York, a sleepy town of 9,000, an hour's drive northwest of New York City.

The miracle cure for my epilepsy, called a lobectomy, is an operation that is still performed in the United States. It has proven effective for thousands of desperate Americans in reducing their epileptic seizures.

My story almost ended before my 12th birthday. At school one day, I began to feel so terribly ill that I could not recall any of the names for the geography test I was taking, though I had carefully learned them all. Of course, the teacher thought I was simply trying to get out of the test, but finally they let me call my parents to tell them to come get me. I simply sat down to wait in a chair in the principal's office, and right then and there, I went into a coma.

Later, my doctors deduced that I had contracted encephalitis, likely from an insect bite gotten when on a horseback riding lesson, but initially they thought that my coma had been induced by a communicable illness. So, when I awoke some nine hours later and found myself in a white room with a cross on the wall, and masked figures hovering over me, I thought either that I was dreaming or that I had died and literally gone to heaven. Of course, many people who lapse into a coma from the brain inflammation of encephalitis do not emerge from it, so I was luckier than some who contract the disease.

By the time New York University Hospital confirmed the diagnosis of encephalitis a week later, I already was having aphasia problems---I simply could not recall words---and from then on, I had regular seizures. The type and frequency of the seizures changed, often due to changes in the medications that they used to try to control the seizures, but I always had to live with the knowledge that I could flip into a seizure with no warning, often in terribly awkward situations.

Over the more than twenty years I endured petit mals, focal seizures, psychomotor seizures, and grand mals, I had learned to hide my affliction from all but my closest friends, even to hide some of its implications from myself. Like many people caught in the inconsistent grip of epilepsy, I paid a large emotional and physical price both from the seizures and from my denial mechanisms.

By the time I was in 7th grade, I had begun to have serious grand mal seizures, and my doctors attempted to control them with medications--dilanthum and phenobarbital at first, and a great many other medications later--but there were times when I would go to the nurse's office and an ambulance would take me to the hospital. Of course, kids being thoughtless kids, I experienced a lot of rejection from my classmates, for like their parents, they knew little about seizures, and I'm sure they were quite frightened by what they saw. Nevertheless, I had to learn how to cope with rejection.

When I went off to college in Massachusetts, things changed for me for the better. People were more mature than my high school classmates had been, and they were more accepting of my illness. But the seizures were getting worse, as petit mals were turning into focal seizures, due at least partly to frequent changes in my medications.

But, for many years, with the help of medications, at least the grand mals subsided.

By the time of my surgery, I had taken eighteen different medications to try to control the seizures, virtually every drug even suspected to control them. Often the combinations of medications I was taking led to changes in the pattern and severity of seizures; frequently, I would end up in the hospital because my body---no human body---can fully adapt to frequent changes in powerful medicines meant to affect the functioning of the brain.

Several seizure-related incidents remain with me as markers on my path toward my miracle surgery.

For instance, while the college I attended assured me that my epilepsy would have no effect on my becoming an elementary school teacher, their institutional assurances crumbled when I had a seizure during student teaching in my senior year. As with all my seizures, I became completely unaware of where I was or what I was doing, so I left my class unattended during the episode. My university not only barred me from further student teaching, it tried to get me to quit school altogether, only relenting after my father came up to Massachusetts to argue my case. They let me graduate, though without my long-sought teaching certification.

And I recall the time when I tried to pay for a newspaper at a Harvard Square newsstand, but my arm was jerking uncontrollably, and I could not talk at all, confusing the poor newspaper seller. Or, after college, the time I was coming home on the subway with another female employee and, during a seizure, I put my hand on her lap. For a while, people at work thought me to be a lesbian. Or the time I had a seizure while trying to put a token in a subway turnstile, a line of irritated New Yorkers waiting impatiently while I repeatedly attempted to insert the coin.

Rejection and embarrassment gave birth to secretiveness: by the time I graduated from college, I had learned to be secretive about my illness, even to myself, so secretive that I nearly killed myself. After college, despite a bout of depression, I managed to find a job working in a nursing home an hour's drive from Port Jervis. While still in high school, I had managed to get through drivers' education classes and obtain my driver's license, despite the fact that I had frequent petit mals while behind the wheel. My stubborn refusal to acknowledge the danger I put myself (and others) in while driving ended in a drive off a steep embankment.

I was returning home from work on a back road when the seizure took hold of my body. When I came to, my car was fifty feet down an embankment, stopped by some trees only a few feet short of a brook. I had whiplash and a few minor scrapes, but God must have been with me, for I could easily have killed myself or somebody else! Shortly thereafter, I moved to New York City, where automobiles are not as essential as in the America of interstate highways.

I found a job in a manufacturing company as an office worker, got married, and settled into what I hoped would be a stable period of my life. Certainly, for ten years, until the company got bought out by another firm, my job was perfect for someone who needed a bit more leeway at times than most people did. The people at my job were terrific: they took care of me when I had seizures, gave me the space to recover from them, and never made me feel unwanted or embarrassed when I would act strangely during a seizure.

Because of their compassion, I was able to handle the pressures and demands of my job. And, for nearly 16 years, my medications had controlled the grand mal seizures.

But things changed. When I thought that I was pregnant, they took me off most of my medications, and the grand mal seizures reasserted themselves. To make emotional matters much worse, I discovered that my husband at the time was having a long-term affair. Although we tried to patch things up through marriage counseling, eventually we went our separate ways. But before then, on a visit to a friend in Boston, the grand mals returned in a particularly embarrassing fashion. At the time I thought I was pregnant, I knew that my husband was cheating on me, and my medications had been radically altered--a perfect combination of factors to bring about a grand mal.

My friend Jill, two of her friends, and I were having dinner in a restaurant when the seizure took me completely by surprise. My friends told me later that I wound up with my face in my plate of food. I was unable to speak at all in the ambulance that took me to the hospital, and for at least three hours afterwards, not even to give rudimentary answers to the doctor's questions. However, I was conscious enough to feel miserable that I was putting my friends through this and that I was once again subject to the unpredictably painful whimsy of grand mal seizures.

The next day, Jill, not one to shrink from a friend's emotional needs, insisted that I go with the group back to the same restaurant. Frightened and embarrassed as I was, I went back, and though I had some minor seizures, we managed this time to finish our meal in a much more conventional manner.

Shortly after my return to New York, the Lord & Taylor incident occurred, and a month later, another grand mal seizure finally pushed me into considering a surgical option that I had rejected years before. I had not been feeling well, and I made an appointment to see a doctor whose office was on the upper East Side of Manhattan, in one of the nicer residential neighborhoods. As I was walking to my appointment, I had a grand mal seizure, falling to the sidewalk, and attracting a crowd of concerned or merely curious people. When I came to, they asked if there was anything that they could do for me, perhaps call an ambulance, but I could not speak, could not walk without tripping over anything in my path, could not get away from the embarrassment of having people watch me in my seizure-caused muteness and clumsiness.

Finally, I recalled why I was in this neighborhood, though I had forgotten the doctor's address and did not think to look in my purse for it, for my thinking patterns were severely affected by this attack. After an hour of walking up and down the street, I was able to find the doctor's office, though I still could not speak coherently. I could not even tell the receptionist what my name was or why I was there. But when the doctor finally examined me, he discovered that I had broken a rib in the incident.

I was seemingly a danger to myself just walking down a peaceful city street, and this steeled my resolve to explore a suggestion that my neurologist had given me several weeks earlier: that I determine whether or not I would be a good candidate for a lobectomy as a last-ditch means of controlling my epilepsy.

Put simply, a lobectomy is an operation to remove a damaged portion of the brain. In most cases, the remaining part of the brain takes up the work load, and the patient returns to normal functioning after a recovery period.

Of course, the idea that I would have part of my brain removed was terrifying, but I knew that I could not go on living with the uncertainty that grand mal seizures brought to my life, unless I had explored all the options for a cure. None of the drugs had stopped my seizures completely, and now I was ready to see if surgery might be the answer.

But there were personal issues complicating matters for me. I was certainly scared, both by the prospect of having part of my brain removed and by my neurologist's warnings that I might have language and short-term memory difficulties after the operation. I worried that I might become a vegetable. To make matters worse, my philandering husband was all for the operation, and I questioned his motives for supporting that course of action. I felt that he was cheating and didn't care about me anymore, didn't care if I became a vegetable or if I died. I did not voice these thoughts to my former husband; rather, I was so desperate that I explored the surgery option.

I met with Dr. Timothy Pedley, a physician at Columbia Presbyterian

Hospital in New York, and formerly chairman of the board of the Epilepsy Foundation of America. He suggested a battery of tests to determine whether I would be a good candidate for surgery, and in June of 1988, I decided to go through with the tests.

Then, my life truly fell apart. In August, after another change in medications left me unable to perform my job, I was fired, leading to a dispute about whether the company would allow me to go on disability. Fortunately, with the help of my neurologist and a labor lawyer, I got the company to reverse its position and put me on disability. Two weeks later, my husband moved out for good.

I was ready for anything, having lost my job, my marriage, and my ability to walk confidently through ordinary reality.

During this time, I managed to calm my fears somewhat, as I located several people who had had the surgery and had fully recovered from it. I discovered that the operation had been successful for half a century, and a couple of the people I met had been seizure-free for more than twenty years. They all seemed to be quite normal, and they all praised the operation as having given them a second chance at a normal life.

I also met with Dr. Neil Schaul, who performed batteries of tests on me, and I met with Sandy Hamburger, a therapist at the Epilepsy Center on Long Island.

They both helped me through some very difficult times of decision and rehabilitation. It turned out that I would be a good candidate for surgery, as the scar tissue from the encephalitis was on the left side of my brain, and this was a good indication that surgery might provide the answer to my seizures.

Since this surgery had been commonly performed in Canada for the prior fifty years, my parents strongly encouraged me to go to Canada to have it done there. But I figured they would have to repeat all the tests I had already been through in New York, and I definitely did not want to go through those tests again.

Finally, my parents and I scheduled a meeting with Dr. Robert Decker, the surgeon who actually performed the operation. And right there in the doctor's waiting room, I had a grand mal seizure, one which broke through my parents' resistance to prompt surgery.

Two weeks later, at Long Island Jewish Hospital, Dr. Decker and his team removed the scarred portion of my brain that was the source of my epileptic seizures. In a little more than a week, I was back at home in Port Jervis, and in three weeks, I returned to my apartment in New York, free of the seizures that had dominated my life for more than two decades.

After the surgery, I did have some complications. The senses on the right side of my body, including taste and touch, were not working properly. Nor did the doctors I consulted know the reason for this. But a woman who was principal of a school for the disabled allayed my worries when she told me that this was quite normal after surgery such as mine, that in a matter of weeks, my senses would return to normal as the right side of the brain compensated for the missing portion of the left side and as the swelling on the left side of my face decreased.

And so it was. After six weeks, everything had returned to normal, to better than my "normal," for I no longer had any seizures whatsoever. No petit mals, no focal seizures, no grand mals. Nor did I experience any language or short-term memory difficulties; in fact, my short-term memory improved, and my general level of intelligence was sharper, probably due to my brain's not having to rejuvenate each time I had a seizure.

I have been free of seizures since this surgery in 1989, and my life has become full once again. I have a successful and fulfilling career in a new field, and I have so many friends and doctors, as well as the Epilepsy Foundation of America, to thank for helping me through my illness and recovery.

In technical terms, note the following:

"Temporal lobectomy is the removal of a portion of the temporal lobe of the brain. It is the most common type of epilepsy surgery and is also the most successful type: After surgery, 60% to 70% of patients are free of seizures that impair consciousness or cause abnormal movements. Some of these patients still experience auras, sensations (odors, for instance) without an outside source.

"20% to 25% of patients still have some complex partial or tonic-clonic seizures, but the number of seizures is reduced by more than 85%.

"10% to 15% of patients have no worthwhile improvement.

"Therefore, more than 85% of patients who have had a temporal lobectomy enjoy a great improvement in seizure control. Most patients need to continue taking seizure medicines, but they usually need less. About 25% of the patients who become seizure-free eventually can stop taking their seizure medicines."

[Source: Howard L. Weiner, MD, and Joseph I. Sirven, MD, http://www.epilepsy.com/learn/treating-seizures-and-epilepsy/surgery/types-surgeries/temporal-lobectomy, August 2013]

For me, this operation was a miracle. None of my fears proved to be true, and all of my hopes were realized. Now, I can walk without fear down whatever streets life takes me to, even down Fifth Avenue, back into Lord & Taylor's jewelry department.

2
Patient Becomes Patient Advocate

"**Qualify life.**" This came from a dream---I have no idea what it was about, but I woke up thinking these words in the middle of the night recently.

After having brain surgery for epilepsy, I decided it was time to change careers. The garment industry was changing. Manufacturing was moving overseas. Department stores in the U.S. were closing: Ohrbach's, Korvettes, Bonwit Teller, Gimbels, B. Altman, Alexander's, Bambergers, Ame's, Abraham & Strauss, Gertz, Stern's, Sibley's, Hills, John Wanamakers. I could keep the listing going, there were so many!

I was seizure-free, hoping to continue to be so for my lifetime. This was the time to begin the new chapter of my life with the possibility of a new career.

When researching the help-wanted ads, I came across an advertisement for customer service. I was interviewed at Empire Blue Cross / Blue Shield. They were interested in hiring me, but felt that I was too experienced and educated to be in customer service. After being interviewed, I was recommended for the claims department at Access America, owned within Blue Cross / Blue Shield by two different groups, BC/BS Empire in New York State and BC/BS in the National Capital area.

Access America was all travel insurance: insurance coverage for trip cancellation, trip interruption, trip delay, baggage loss, baggage

| 11

delay, emergency evacuation, funeral expenses, hijacking, repatriation of remains and a few other coverages. I supervised claims adjustment in all aspects of travel insurance coverage, administered the payout function of all claims, managed all investigation and research performed by six examiners, interacted with clients, travel agents, World Access (assistance service), and other travel and medical service providers and trained examiners to analyze claims and obtain additional documentation to complete claimants' files for accurate adjudication. I also handled claims involving credit card fraud.

After being a claims examiner for one month, I became a claims supervisor. At first, I would try to find out if a claim was covered. I was immediately taught to look at the exclusions to see if there was a way to deny the claim according to the exclusions in the policy.

I was taught to deny claims. This happened at two insurance companies where I worked. I also learned what made the insurance company change decisions involving a denial. I handled all the irate phone calls. Every day, insured clients called about their denials, and I handled each and every appeal and complaint phone call. It was quite heartbreaking. But I learned the tricks of the trade.

After working almost two years at Access America, I joined American International Group. I began as a Senior Claims Analyst and investigated, evaluated, and processed personal effects resulting in a 50% savings to AIG. I managed and rectified relationships with a $1M account (British Universities North America Club), significantly increasing client satisfaction, and aided the underwriters/legal department on redesigning policy provisions and definitions.

My next position at American International Group was as Leisure Travel Insurance Administrator, where I issued policies and proposals and made contract changes, reviewed and prepared solicitation material, obtained legal sign-off, analyzed new submissions, including comparison of pricing to similar in-force accounts, calculated Managing General Agent's expenses and separated them into appropriate insurance coverage categories and reviewed monthly claim reports, verifying that expenses/losses were charged properly. At that point I was learning the premiums, losses, and expenses in all areas of the insurance industry.

My last corporate position was in entertainment underwriting at American International Group, where I underwrote and priced all types of entertainment insurance including Package, General Liability, Automobile, Workers' Compensation, and Umbrella Coverage, reviewed new and renewal submissions and obtained additional data from brokers, prepared presentations for management regarding information on new/renewal policies, communicated and documented acceptances and declinations to brokers and verified premium and loss data and reviewed contract wording for accuracy.

At this point, I felt well-rounded. I truly understood the insurance industry.

After working at both insurance companies for over 10 years, I briefly worked at a local insurance agency. I took off awhile after adopting my two children in Vietnam, and I kept my feet wet by being active in the Insurance Professionals of Orange County, NY.

I approached one of my own doctors about handling all of his medical bills, submitting them to the insurance company. While working for the doctor, I learned what the insurance companies required to get the providers' claims paid. Even on the medical specialists' side, the insurance companies don't want to pay the claims. Most health insurance companies provide very little information to the medical provider on what information must be submitted on their bills, so the insurance company can either deny or suspend the claim. Any delay allows the insurance companies to hold on to the premium and save money.

I worked with this doctor for several years. At one point, I was working for four different providers and handling their credentialing with the insurance companies. Credentialing is a process used to evaluate the qualifications and practice history of a doctor. This process includes a review of a doctor's completed education, training, residency and licenses. It also includes any certifications issued by a board in the doctor's area of specialization. Due to insurance companies' paying out so little money to the medical providers, **I learned that the bigger the group of practitioners, the more they can demand from the insurance company.** For that reason, as well as for very high medical liability coverage for providers, many doctors have now joined large groups of physicians or have become hospitalists, employees of hospitals.

I was at a point where people kept coming to me for help with their claims. I was inspired to open MedWise Insurance Advocacy, a division of MedWise Billing, Inc., after someone I knew had a case coming up in court with which he asked for help because he felt that the bills that Medicare had paid and was requesting restitution for if he won the case, were not all related to his injury. I spent many hours on his case, but when completed, **I reduced his reimbursement to Medicare from $106,000 to $22,000. That inspired my opening MedWise Insurance Advocacy, a division of MedWise Billing, Inc.**

Through my years of experience at the insurance companies and by owning a medical billing company, **I realized I now knew what makes the insurance companies tick and how to help everyone with denied, overcharged, out-of-network, and other going-nowhere claims.**

After working with so many heart-wrenching cases and learning about people dying due to not receiving treatment or medication, I hold the health insurance advocacy business very close to my heart.

3
Diagnosing and Reducing Your Medical Bills

Based on my own medical issues and professional experience handling insurance matters, I [AGG] experienced just how complex, stressful, and confusing medical bills, Explanations of Benefits (EOBs), and medical codes can be, and I decided I wanted to help people in this area.

Unfortunately, stress caused by trying to figure out your health insurance is not covered!

This chapter consists of various topics, guidance, and suggestions to potentially reduce your medical expenses.

How to Cut Your Medical Bills

Know your rights / be aware of your medical benefits.

It is not an easy task to understand your medical bills and the Explanation of Benefits. But to know your rights and be aware of your medical benefits, you must scrutinize your medical insurance policy.

Know what you are covered for and what your exclusions are. Exclusions in an insurance policy list what you are *not* covered for.

Call the hospital and medical providers. Check to see what the fees will be. Also check the Internet to see what your doctor's rating was for this disease.

Is This Test Required? Why Is This Test Required? Save Money!

One cartoonist depicted a doctor examining a patient who is hooked up to an elaborate piece of medical instrumentation: "First, we're going to run some tests to help pay off the machine."

Sometimes, especially if you feel that you are being over-tested or charged too much money for a procedure, ask the medical provider, "What options might be less expensive to get the information you need to accurately diagnose my problem?"

If a doctor is recommending a test, it is best to call your health insurance carrier and ask whether the test might require pre-approval. An example is an endoscopy.

Make sure your doctor or hospital has pre-approval before the procedure is performed.

Also make sure by contacting the insurance carrier that the medical provider has a contract with your insurance carrier. I also recommend that you ask for this in writing. I hear so many cases where the provider's office states that there has been an approval or the medical provider verbally informs you that they have a contract with your health insurance carrier, and they do not.

If you are about to have surgery and pre-tests are required before the main procedure, make sure your health insurance carrier has agreed to the services and that it has a contract with the pre-test companies. Location of services and medical provider must both be approved.

Ask the provider if you are required to have someone drive you home after the procedure.

If you learn that multiple tests are not required, you will save money. On the other hand **if multiple tests are required, it is best to have them performed on the same day and location.** Many medical providers are against that since they are able to make more money if the procedures are on different dates. One of the major reasons for the Affordable Care Act (ACA) was to require all hospitals and medical providers to share medical information via electronic medical records, hopefully reducing the number of duplicated tests.

Many insurance companies hire an outside company that does the approval for pre-certification.

If you are informed that the medical provider is not approved, ask your health insurance carrier who the approval company is and if they know which other doctors the pre-cert company might approve.

Perhaps it goes without saying that you will also try to assure yourself of the qualifications of the doctor whom you are seeing, to avoid the situation depicted by a cartoonist who showed one patient saying to another, "Yes – that's my surgeon – the one who cuts himself shaving.…"

As an example of the peculiarities of some coverages, if you have a tetanus shot, you may be covered only once every 10 years. If the insurance carrier does not have record of the last tetanus shot, they may want to deny the bill for the tetanus shot until you can prove that you did not have the tetanus shot during the last 10 years. The insurance company may deny the claim if your last shot was less than 10 years ago, or if you are unable to provide them with information as to when you had your last tetanus shot.

For another example, if you are on Medicare and are about to be transported via ambulance, the only way you are potentially covered is if you are taken to the ambulance by stretcher. Such trips can cost hundreds of dollars.

Options for the Uninsured and Underinsured

Medicare has an 80/20 agreement; therefore, if you have a hospital bill of $30,000, do you want to be responsible for 20% of the $30,000, which is $6,000? That is the reason why, **if you are able to afford it, if is often best to have either basic Medicare with supplementary health insurance coverage or one of the Medicare Advantage Plans, which often have rules different from the 80/20 rule.**

If your employer offers a plan, find out what you are covered for and determine whether you would want additional health insurance through your spouse or partner. Also, discuss with your and / or your spouse's employer what options are available to you. Sometimes they might have different insurance carriers to choose from or different levels of coverage. If there is no coverage, contact the state to see what it might offer. For example, in New York State, go to https://nystateofhealth.ny.gov/

Medicare Advantage Plans are health plans that are approved by Medicare and provided by private companies. Medicare sets the rules for Medicare Advantage Plans and regulates the private companies who operate the Plans. See our chapter on these plans.

Medicare Advantage Plans cover Medicare Part A and Part B, sometimes including vision and dental care. You pay a copay and/or a deductible; you still pay your Medicare premium and might need to also pay an additional premium.

Typically you are required to see the plan's network doctors and you cannot buy a Medicare supplement to help pay out-of-pocket expenses.

Sometimes it is advantageous to go out of the United States for medical care, but precautions need to be taken.

Medical Tourism

Should you seek bargains in medical and dental care by going outside the US? There are plenty of bargains if you decide to have dental work or surgery outside of the US. The reasons why most people will travel out of the US for dental or surgery (such surgery usually being face lifts or liposuction) include:

1. You have a critical medical problem causing a large co-pay.
2. Your elective surgery is not being covered.
3. If you need a transplant, you might have a lesser waiting period.

4. You like the idea of combining medical treatment with a semi-vacation in an attractive area.
5. Some insurance companies suggest foreign treatment due to the fees---believe it or not!
6. There are treatments that you can receive overseas but not approved or available in the US.

Medical tourism is a thriving business. According to Deloitte Consulting, the number of Americans traveling for medical care is around 800,000 per year. You can, for instance, take a trip to Costa Rica, Brazil, Thailand, or South Africa for much cheaper procedures than down the road at your local hospital. Dental treatment is available in Mexico, Central America and Eastern Europe, which have major centers for foreign dental work. Surgery is provided in over 40 countries, e.g., Argentina, Austria, the United Arab Emirates, Vietnam, Central America, Southeast Asia and Eastern Europe. Done correctly and safely, having dental work or surgery overseas can save you up to 90%.

But before you buy your plane ticket, serious and careful research is important to make sure you don't get trapped in a *60 Minutes* black market surgery sting: "Check to see if your insurance company will provide medical evacuation from a foreign country due to elective surgery gone wrong and if your insurance carrier will pay for care necessary due to complications from foreign elective procedures. Chances are good that electing to have treatment abroad will not be approved by your insurance carrier in advance; non-emergency procedures you have abroad may void your insurance carrier's obligations to pay for your follow-up care in the US."

You can always investigate the overseas services by contacting the American Medical Association, the Joint Commission International based in the U.S. or the British based QHA Trent.

Being a wise consumer of medical services also requires looking to reduce the cost of your prescription medicines, discussed next.

Take a look at the Costco Drug Plan on the web. It is called The Costco Member Prescription Program (CMPP). Costco drugs must be purchased either on line or by phone from their pharmacy in Everett, Washington. You have access to the Costco pharmacy without being a member of Costco. You just cannot go to your local pharmacy to purchase the Costco medications. They need to be ordered online or by phone. Check with the state/county to see what might be free or discounted through the state.

Another option besides Costco is the site pharmacychecker.com or CIPA, the Canadian International Pharmacy Association. A full list of CIPA members is available to assist you in finding a safe online source for your prescription medications.

Drugs from Canada

Drugs are imported from all over the world. Drugs sold through Canada are carefully checked. When you go online, put in your drugs and dosage. When ordering your drugs through Canada, a prescription is required by reputable firms.

When searching online, you will see that the website will say, "It is illegal to buy drugs from another country even for your own use; HOWEVER, the United States Government has never prosecuted anyone for ordering 90 days or less for your own use."

Drugs from Mexico

Many years ago, I was in Nogales, Mexico, while visiting a dear friend who had moved to Tucson, AZ, due to severe asthma. When I was returning to Arizona with asthma medication for my friend, the U.S. security guard asked me what I purchased. I showed him this bag of medications, and he began laughing at me. The reason he was laughing was because of my honesty involving the amount of medicine I purchased. He said that no one is ever honest with him and shows all the medications bought.

Don't Assume Your Bill Is Correct / How Medical Bills Came into Being

Medical bills can be shocking. One cartoonist showed a patient in bed with a doctor at the bedside saying, "I'll have someone come in and prep you for the bill."

It has been estimated that 80% of medical bills contain errors, so checking your bill is important.

Many years ago, prior to 1966, you would see a doctor and pay a flat fee. Doctors used to be able to bill whatever they felt like billing. Every year health insurance carriers have become stricter on their payouts.

Now, when you see a doctor for multiple conditions, you will have multiple procedure codes on your bill.

Tiered Payments

What this means to you as a consumer: the health insurance carrier pays 100% of the allowable amount for the procedure code incurring the highest fee. For the procedure code incurring the second-highest fee during the same visit, the provider will receive 50% of the allowable amount. For the third-highest fee for a different procedure code, during the same visit, the provider will receive 25% of the allowable amount. If the provider is out-of-network, you might be responsible for the difference of what was paid and what was not.

A physician assisting the primary physician will receive a lesser percentage than the primary physician if the insurance company is billed for the same procedure codes by the assisting physician.

Current Procedural Terminology (CPT®) codes were developed by the American Medical Association and first published in 1966.

ICD-9 codes began in May 1976. In October, 2015, ICD-10 came into play.

ICD-10 has 141,000 codes—more than 8 times the 17,000 codes in ICD-9. The additional codes enable practices to be more specific on claim forms in reporting the care provided to patients. My fear is if your medical provider is not up to date with the ICD-10 codes that began October 1, 2015, your claims could be denied.

Health Insurance Portability and Accountability Act of 1996: Privacy

HIPAA mandates all health insurance companies that are covered entities make the transition to ICD-10. Workers' compensation and property and casualty insurance companies are not covered entities.

For example, I see a new doctor for the first time due to a cold. The procedure code is 99201 (new patient, office visit), the ICD-9 code is 460 and the ICD-10 code is J00, a cold. I go back to the doctor a few days later due to conjunctivitis, the procedure code is 99211, established patient; the ICD-10 code is H10.

What this means to all of us is that as of October 1, 2015, if your diagnosis does not begin with a letter, question your doctor, otherwise your insurance company will deny the claim.

ICD-10 codes are available on: http://www.cms.gov/icd10

CPT codes are available on: http://www.reference.com/motif/business/free-cpt-code-lookup

One Visit – Ten Bills – WHY?

When you go to an emergency room or are a patient at a hospital, you will almost always see multiple bills, whether you are in a room at the hospital as an inpatient or in the emergency room.

Here are some of the bills that you will see separately billed:

1. Hospitalist Bill – Hospitalist is a doctor who works for the hospital
2. Emergency Room Doctor Bill
3. Cardiologist Bill

4. Plastic Surgeon Bill
5. Pathologist Bill
6. Lab Bill
7. X-Ray Bill
8. Radiology Bill
9. Room and Board
10. Fee for Emergency Room
11. Fee for Operating Room
12. Fee for Blood Work
13. Fee to Read Blood Work Scan
14. Medication Fee
15. CT Scan Fee
16. MRI Fee

Who Is Processing Your Medical Bill?

Many hospitals and individual doctors hire outside companies to handle all of their medical bills. Either the bill is handled by the medical provider, hospital, doctor, laboratory company or it is sent to an outside medical billing company that is hired by the medical provider.

Where do problems occur?

The problems occur if the billing company or the medical practice:

1. does not handle any of the follow-ups,
2. does not submit the bills to your secondary or tertiary insurer,
3. is incompetent to bill correctly,
4. sends your medical bills to overseas medical billing companies,
5. does not have the prior pre-approval for the necessary procedures,
6. makes errors with pre-authorization, or
7. if the bills are not submitted within the insurance company's allowed time period.

How to Decode the Bill?

Most of the bills are now submitted electronically and when done so, the same information that is on a CMS 1500 form is required.

What to Do with the Bill Once Decoded? Is the Bill within Reasonable and Customary Charges?

All bills, when paid by Medicare, Medicaid or a Commercial Health Insurance Carrier are determined according to procedure codes. Commercial Insurers follow Medicare except normally on a higher payout percentage.

Medicare and Medicaid also add a Diagnosis Related Group code, called a DRG code, when determining the payment for hospitalization as an inpatient.

To find the Medicare Allowable Usual, Reasonable and Customary codes, look at the Medicare website. You will find the listings under:
http://www.cms.gov/apps/physician-fee-schedule/

Appropriate Usage for GY Code

If the services provided are under statutory exclusion from the Medicare program, then the claim would be denied whether or not the modifier is present on the claim. It is not necessary to provide the patient with an ABN, Advance Beneficiary Notice, for these situations:

1. Situations excluded based on a section of the Social Security Act
2. Modifier GY will cause the claim to be denied, with the patient liable for the charges.

Inappropriate Usage for GY Code

1. Do not use on bundled procedures
2. Do not use on add-on codes

With GY Code, the medical provider who submits the claim to Medicare is telling Medicare, "Don't Pay It!"

Taking Action in Order to Decrease Your Bill

1. If your hospitalization is not an emergency, check your insurance policy to interpret your coverage. Take a good look at the coverages and exclusions on your policy.
2. Call the hospital's billing department and ask what the room charges are and just what they cover. An example is, let's say tissues are not included, bring your own.
3. Ask your doctor to estimate the cost of your treatment. Ask if the hospital will allow you to bring your own prescription drugs.
4. Make sure that all the providers who will be treating you are on your health insurance plan.
5. If you are able, keep a log of all your tests, medication and treatments. If you are not able to, then ask a friend or relative to help you.
6. Make sure you do not throw out your Explanation of Benefits [EOB] from your health insurance carrier. It often says "this is not a bill." Your EOB, will provide you with: the monies charged by the provider, how much money was paid by your insurance carrier, how much your deductible was and what your copay amount should be.
7. Never pay your hospital bill before leaving the hospital. Even if the hospital is telling you it is required.
8. When your bill arrives, read it carefully. Compare it to the log you have from the hospital along with the EOB and the estimate of charges you had requested prior to entering the hospital.
9. If you do not understand your bills, call the billing department and your insurer and request an explanation. Don't accept

bills that say "lab fees" or "miscellaneous fees," unless you have a further description.

The Buck Stops Here

Fight and never be afraid. If you disagree with the bill, fight it before you pay it.

Tying It All Together

1. Know Your Rights - Be Aware of Your Medical Benefits.
2. Don't You Just Love a Bargain? Compare Prices for Tests at Hospitals and Medical Facilities.
3. Ask the Right Questions.
4. Check Options for the Medically Uninsured and Underinsured – Call Your State Department of Insurance.
5. Look for Discounts on Your Medication.
6. Don't Assume Your Bill Is Correct.
7. Check All Your Medical Bills for One Visit and Make Sure You Were Not Overcharged.
8. Determine Who is Processing Your Medical Bill.
9. Learn How to Decode Your Bill.
10. Make Sure the Bill is Within Reasonable and Customary Charges.
11. Take Action In Order To Decrease Your Bill.
12. Fight It Before You Pay It, and Never Be Afraid!

Yes, we have repeated ourselves, because some things definitely bear repetition.

Catching the Errors

Decoding your hospital bill may seem like a daunting task but it's definitely worth the effort. Studies have shown that hospital billing errors cause patients to be overcharged an average of $1,300 per stay.

Here are some tips to help you get started:

1. Request a daily itemized bill and review it thoroughly. You can't catch errors if you don't know specifically what you're being charged for.
2. Make sure you're charged for the correct length of stay and the right kind of room. Note that most insurance companies do not allow hospitals to charge for your discharge day, although many hospitals frequently do so anyway.
3. Watch for double billing - being charged for the same service twice. This is the most common mistake hospitals make.
4. Check for phantom charges. Many hospitals have a set of standard fees for certain procedures that they automatically charge, even though the doctor canceled it.
5. Look for overpriced extras. Some hospitals may charge for extra supplies like towels, gloves or a box of tissue, which should all be included in the room charge. Also check medication charges. Were you charged $10 for a pill that would have cost you $1 to buy yourself?
6. Check operating room time. It's not uncommon for hospitals to bill for more time than you actually used. Compare the charge with your anesthesiologist's records.
7. If you do find errors or have questions regarding your bill, talk with your doctor or contact the hospital's billing office or patient representative. If the bill has already been sent to the insurer, call your insurance agent.
8. Watch your deductible. Insurance companies have been known to mistakenly charge you long after you've met your deductible. File away every bill you pay, and watch for charges above your deductible.

4
Hospital Over-Charges

Ask These Five Questions about Medical Expenses to Avoid Over-Paying

Consumers should ask five questions before blindly paying a medical bill to make sure they are receiving the proper reimbursements or are not being overcharged or incorrectly billed.

People don't realize that an incorrect diagnostic code will cause the insurance company to deny a claim, or that there might be charges on a bill for services not actually rendered. People should read those statements carefully and ask themselves or their providers several questions that can save them a lot of money.

1. **Is the statement fully itemized?**
   Look for dates of service for each office visit and/or procedure or test, with the provider's charges and any insurance payments applied to the bill. Do not accept a statement with only total charges and total amount owed on it. If an itemized medical bill is not received, contact the provider's billing department and request one.

2. **Are the billed services the ones you received?**
   Human and machine errors do occur, and treatments, visits,

or tests could be duplicated by mistake. Of course, there is a chance that the incorrect billing was intentional, so read the itemizations carefully and don't be afraid to speak up. Examples of billing errors include billing for a private hospital room when the patient was in a shared room or being billed for a test that was canceled before it was administered. Whether or not there is a suspicion of foul play, always keep a record of procedures, treatments and office visits as a proactive measure.

3. **Do the charges align with the EOB?**
   The insurance company will issue an Explanation of Benefits (EOB) after processing a claim. The EOB will show what the insurer considers "reasonable and customary" fees for various services, how much went towards the deductible, what was covered, and what the patient might still owe the provider. Double-check the EOB against the medical bills received for any outstanding balance to make sure that all charges are correct and that potential overspending is curbed.

   Many people are overwhelmed by the paperwork, and become confused about what their health insurance really covers or what's considered in-network or out-of-network.

4. **Is all the identification information correct?**
   Consumers should insure that the name, address, and health insurance policy numbers are all correct, as well as the contact information and insurance numbers for the physician or facility. If the consumer has changed health insurance, that person should provide an update to the healthcare provider and have the billing department re-submit it to the correct insurance company.

5. **Were the correct CPT codes used?**
   The CPT codes—or current procedural terminology codes—must be correct and must indicate medical services that the policy covers in order for the claim to be processed rather than rejected. These codes apply to both diagnosis and treatment. The American Medical Association's website has a CPT guide consumers can use.

Anyone who suspects fraudulent or incorrect charges or has been denied insurance coverage he or she should get according to their policy may dispute the bill or the EOB. For many people, the correspondence with the insurance company and medical provider can be daunting and the paperwork confusing, which is where medical insurance advocates can help.

MedWise is often contacted by individuals or their families to help figure out what they really owe, and to resubmit claims to insurers or talk to the medical provider about reducing fees for procedures that are not covered. It is very gratifying when MedWise Insurance Advocacy can help someone who's recovering from an illness or surgery by relieving that stress during a sensitive time.

5
Successful Challenges

Patient Beware—and Be Informed!

Imagine being that patient who has had the procedure completed at the hospital and is now advised, "Yes, you were admitted to the hospital, but you were admitted as an outpatient (under observation) and not as an inpatient."

This situation is not only extremely confusing and upsetting for the patient, it has major ramifications for Medicare coverage. As an outpatient, the patient is going to be responsible to pay for:

1. Hospital room and board.
2. Medications.
3. Rehabilitation/skilled nursing fees if they end up going to a rehab facility after leaving the hospital. Rehabilitation daily fees often range between $400 to $800 a day, not including additional fees for physical therapy, speech therapy and/or occupational therapy.

Within a three-day period, MedWise Insurance Advocacy had two different cases related to this topic directed to their office. With the first case, the patient was still in the hospital and they were able to have the hospital change their status from "admitted outpatient, under observation" to "admitted inpatient." This averted great financial burden.

In the second case, it was too late to request an alteration. Prior to the hospitalization, the patient was informed he was going to be **admitted**. By the time he realized he was admitted as an "outpatient" he had been discharged from the hospital for five days, was about to leave a rehab facility, and was now required to pay the full rehab bill before being released. Since this client was already out of the hospital it was impossible to revise the hospital status of "outpatient admitted" to "inpatient admitted."

What are the hospitals' plans to clarify the information they are giving the patient prior to admittance? This lack of transparency is unsettling to say the least. Many patients with a limited budget cannot afford the astronomical fees. They were never pre-informed nor were they prepared to pay these expensive (and unexpected) hospital and rehab fees. If a patient is not covered for Part A and does not have a supplement for Medicare, he or she will be covered for Part B (outpatient) at only 80% out of the 100% allowed rate.

Confronting the Admissions Confusion

Hospitals must put clear communication with patients about their admission status and Medicare coverage at the top of any treatment plan. Patients and their families must be aware of the potential for the confusion about how they are being admitted—"inpatient admittance" or "outpatient admittance"—and ask questions of their physicians or hospitals either before or upon being admitted to the hospital.

Find out if subsequent sub-acute care will be covered and if the three-night minimum inpatient stay is being met. It is already difficult enough having to go through medical procedures or surgeries; there is no reason to further compound the situation by discovering that Medicare and some commercial insurers won't cover hospital stays or rehabilitative treatment because of inpatient vs. outpatient status.

Insurance Advocacy Saved a Client $98,000 in Medical Expenses

The grown daughter of a senior citizen contacted an elder law attorney after seeing her mother's enormous medical bills following two hospitalizations and stays in rehabilitation centers. The bills—from 13 different healthcare providers—totaled $100,000. Due to the overwhelming paperwork, the daughter did not have the time to go through all of them properly to track what her mother truly owed, and turned to the elder law attorney for advice.

The attorney called me [AGG] for help sorting through all the medical bills and ascertaining the family's true out-of-pocket medical costs. I contacted each of the 13 healthcare providers and facilities and negotiated the bills with all of them. I worked out payment terms with each provider that allowed the client to pay a reduced amount on some; on others, I discovered where Medicare coverage should have been extended and negotiated coverage as well as discounts.

In the end, the patient wound up having to pay only $2000 out of the original $100,000.

Although this story has a happy ending, unfortunately, amassing enormous medical bills is an all-too-common occurrence. As a medical bill insurance advocate, I have been helping people with the burden of medical bills.

A Nursing Home's Collections Case Became a Big Refund for the Client Instead

A family contacted MedWise Insurance Advocacy in 2011 while they were in collections with a nursing facility in New York for $20,000. When the advocacy work was completed, the family received a large refund for overpayment instead.

Their elderly mother had been in the nursing home for almost five months, during which time the family had paid $29,000, and the Medicare Advantage plan paid $56,000. The home was trying to collect an additional $20,000 from the family. This amount totaled $105,000 ($21,000 a month). However, the normal rates for a skilled nursing facility range from $8,000 to $12,000 a month; therefore, the bill at that point should not have been more than $60,000.

I [AGG] wrote letters to the NYS Attorney General and NYS Consumer Affairs, which sent the case to Medicare in NYC. Medicare in NYC contacted the Medicare Advantage Plan, which paid an additional $15,000 to the nursing home (leaving a $5,000 balance in collections).

I made numerous phone calls to the nursing home's accounting department to work out the amount owed, as well as work through the confusion of who owned the facility. I was able to verify ownership and contacted the owner to discuss the case. Through negotiations, MedWise Insurance Advocacy was able to secure a refund for overpayment of $16,000. **In short, the family, who began with a collections bill for $20,000, wound up being refunded over $16,000.**

Advocating for Access to Information the Health Facility Denied the Patient

A student in a New York City college got appendicitis and ended up in a NYC hospital. After multiple, unsuccessful attempts to obtain an itemized bill from the hospital, the student's family came to MedWise Insurance Advocacy for help. The hospital's billing office would not provide the family with the itemized bill, which the health insurance company requires for reimbursement. I [AGG] contacted the hospital CEO's office and worked with the CEO's administrative assistant, who helped the student get the itemized bill.

Explore How Initial Claim Was Prepared and Filed, Understand What Is Covered in Your Health Plans

As many people discover with their health plans, there is a strong possibility the insurance company will look for a way to reject a claim. We advise patients that when they receive a claim rejection, they should carefully review their Explanations of Benefits to make sure the health care providers have properly filed the claim.

The more that people understand how the medical insurance system works, and the recourse they have, the more success they will have in getting the health coverage and medical reimbursements they deserve. It's important that individuals really understand what all these plans cover and how to best work with the insurance company in order to avoid huge, unexpected out-of-pocket expenses. Here are several important tips on how to reduce the odds that a health insurance claim will be rejected, and what to do in case that happens:

1. **Understand your medical insurance policy.** Know in advance what is considered non-emergency medical care, what you will pay for unusual or out-of-the-ordinary treatments, and which providers are in network and out of network. Read your benefits manual and ask questions.
2. **Get preauthorization from your insurer.** For medical procedures that are beyond a typical office visit, get the go-ahead from the insurance company first to avoid huge out-of-pocket expenses or a bureaucratic runaround. Have this preauthorization sent to you in writing to prevent the insurer from later denying your claim.
3. **Ask your doctor to submit a letter.** If your insurer will not preauthorize a procedure, do not assume this rejection is final. Ask your doctor to submit a letter to the insurer explaining why the procedure is required in your case.
4. **Be persistent.** If preauthorization is again denied, ask your doctor to try again, this time describing your health situation and the necessity of the procedure in greater detail. Insurers often back down when patients and doctors persist. If a medical claim has been rejected, do not pay it right away but

rather, investigate why the insurer did not cover it the first time. Several issues may be in play.

5. **Incorrect billing codes.** An incorrect procedure or diagnostic code by the healthcare provider will get the claim kicked out. If this is the case, ask the provider's billing department to resubmit the bill to your insurer with the correct codes.
6. **Billed under the wrong insurance policy.** Confirm that the policy number and/or group number on the paperwork corresponds with your current policy, and if not, have the billing office resubmit the claim correctly.
7. **The insurer continues billing you after you've met your deductible and/or out-of-pocket maximum.** Keep a file each year of your medical bills and your Explanations of Benefits (EOBs) to track your expenses. Compare your records against those of the insurer and find out why its tally doesn't match yours. Keep in mind that the insurer may not count the full amounts charged by out-of-network providers.

When a medical claim is denied, employ these steps that individuals can perform on their own or hire a medical insurance advocate to do them:

1. **Get on the phone.** If it is not clear why the insurer rejected a claim, call the customer service department and ask for a clear explanation of why. Ask to speak to a supervisor if you don't agree with, or don't understand, the answer, or call back repeatedly until you get a representative who will explain it clearly. Document your calls and take notes. Individuals under group coverage should contact their plan administrator or human resources representative for negotiating assistance.
2. **Contact your Department of Aging or similar agency,** if you

are age 65 or older, to request assistance if you cannot get resolution on your own.
3. **Ask your state's Department of Insurance for guidance**. Often the regulators are very aggressive and helpful in getting insurers that are licensed by the state to pay—sometimes with interest.

If you or the people helping you are unable to manage this process, hire a claims-assistance professional. Professionals are listed on the National Association of Healthcare Advocacy Consultants website (NAHAC.com) or the Alliance of Claims Assistance Professionals (Claims.org).

A professional medical insurance advocate understands state insurance laws and policy details and will make all contacts up the insurance hierarchy and, if necessary, up the legislative chain to Congress. Advocates relieve the stress of this process by working with the insurance company to get your legitimate claims covered and get the reimbursements you deserve, or negotiate down your medical bills with the billing departments and insurance companies.

A Medical Insurance Advocate Can Help You Recoup Money You Are Owed, and Keep You from Paying What You Don't Owe

Regardless of how good your health insurance plan is, you are bound to bump up against issues regarding payments for services you thought were covered, overpayments, wrongful billing, and denied medical claims at least once in your life.

Many baby boomers are also confronting their aging parents' mounting medical needs, healthcare costs, and navigating the murky waters of Medicare, Medicaid, secondary insurers, and ignored medical bills. Depending on their age, they could also be dealing with these issues for themselves.

Working with a medical insurance advocate can relieve a lot of this burden, and provide much-needed support to individuals and families who are fighting with their health insurance carriers or healthcare providers over medical bills and claims—or simply need help wading through, organizing, and prioritizing a growing mountain of them. Even if you are well, as a busy entrepreneur or business owner your mind is on other matters related to your business—not on figuring out if you paid too much, if your coverage is right, or if that denied medical claim has merit.

What a Medical Insurance Advocate Does

Let's face it: when someone is dealing with an illness or recovering from surgery, and those bills start flowing in from multiple physicians, hospitals, and rehab centers, it doesn't take long for the situation to become overwhelming and confusing. Sorting through the Explanations of Benefits and trying to understand exactly what is covered and what is not—often revealed once those unexpected charges come through—can become a burden very quickly.

Insurance advocates act as the expert liaisons between patients and providers. They work with patients regarding their health insurance coverage, medical bills and claims, and can handle all communication and paperwork with the insurance carriers as well as medical facilities or service providers. They are the bridge between patients and health insurance companies, acting on their clients' behalf to get claims passed, to ensure the highest coverage allowed (depending on the health plan), and to enable patients and their families to rest easy, knowing their insurance matters are in expert hands.

Many medical insurance advocates also work with elder law and personal injury attorneys to make sure that all their clients' medical claims are processed and paid correctly.

These experienced professionals sort through and resolve clients' medical bills, lien claims, insurance pre-authorizations, denied medical claims, and medical letters of appeal. They can explain those bewildering Explanations of Benefits and advocate for patients regarding any insurance issues that require expert or objective attention.

MedWise is a business and we need to charge fees. The charges are determined either by percentage, hourly rate, or hourly rate plus percentage. Every case is different.

Before You Pay Those Medical Bills . . .

The onus is definitely on the patient or patient's family when it comes to medical bills, and there's no question that following the audit trail can quickly become baffling. A few precautionary measures are advised to protect you. A medical insurance advocate can also perform these steps for you:

1. Before services are rendered, be sure that all the medical providers accept your health insurance.
2. If the medical provider does not accept health insurance, see if there is a way you can agree to a reasonable fee for the services before rendered and obtain the agreement in writing.
3. When receiving a bill from a hospital/healthcare facility, a physician or other healthcare provider, from a lab, or bills for medical tests, verify that:
   a. All of the services were actually rendered and
   b. The medical provider is not charging above the usual, reasonable, and customary fees.
4. Be sure that all of the services are listed clearly and distinctly on the bill with an explanation of the services, including the five-digit CPT (Current Procedural Terminology) codes.
5. If you disagree with any of the charges from the medical providers, ask for an explanation in writing from them.
6. Be sure there are no duplicate charges for the service fees on the medical bills.

Hire a Medical Insurance Advocate? Eight Good Reasons Why You Should

Health insurance carriers are not infallible; nor are they as monolithic as many consumers are led to believe. In the hands of the right professional, you can achieve results, whether it's simply a matter of ascertaining medical fees or fighting a denial. Some reasons to engage a medical insurance advocate are:

1. You believe you were overcharged for a procedure, exam, tests, or a hospital/rehab stay.
2. You are having trouble determining the correct fees.
3. You are unable to reach a human being from the provider's office who can help you.
4. You are unable to handle the medical bill case alone.
5. A medical claim you expected to be covered was denied.
6. The health insurance carrier has decided to take the medical provider's reimbursement back due to an error, and now you are expected to pay the difference.
7. You are uninsured or not covered for a specific medical procedure.
8. The doctor, hospital, or other medical provider does not accept health insurance.

Turning Ten Denials into More Than $40,000

I [AGG] was contacted by a New York resident who was unable to get the proper reimbursement from his health insurance for services rendered two years before. The patient hired MedWise after six denials of his medical claim by his insurance carrier. After several attempts to get the client the reimbursement he deserved, I filed his case with the New York State Department of Financial Services. The agency overturned the denials and instructed the insurance company to pay the money to my client.

1. I worked with Medicare and the patient's secondary private health insurance carrier to ascertain actual medical costs and establish the denials.
2. I worked through three subsequent denials and then wrote to and appealed the case with New York State's Department of Insurance, Department of Financial Services, Department of Consumer Affairs, and the state's Attorney General.
3. I sent a copy of the letter to the health insurance carrier, who denied the claim a tenth time.
4. Through my repeated efforts, the NYS Department of Financial Services reversed the denial and **the insurance company reimbursed my client over $40,000—his original $35,000 out-of-pocket costs plus interest.**

Fight Insurance Companies and Medical Providers on Contested Charges, Confusing Bills

At a time when the health insurance industry is under government scrutiny, healthcare costs are skyrocketing, and consumers are becoming more aware of their patient rights, patients need to be vigilant about their medical bills. For those with medical insurance, but who are facing inadequate coverage or insurance company loopholes, a medical insurance advocate provides valuable assistance recouping unwarranted expenses.

MedWise Insurance Advocacy has achieved extraordinary results for its clients by working out highly beneficial arrangements for those who have exhausted all other avenues. Since founding my practice in January 2012, MedWise firm has recovered approximately $5,000,000 in medical expenses that insurers have tried to block or that healthcare providers erroneously charged.

When people are sick or in recovery from an illness or surgery, the last thing they want to do is fight the insurance company or physician about their medical expenses; nor are they equipped to manage the intricacies of the health insurance industry. As a medical insurance advocate, I am the liaison between patient or attorney, insurance company, and medical provider who works out a solution that resolves billing disputes. In addition to working with individuals, I handle cases for elder law and personal injury attorneys.

Medical Insurance Advocacy Cases

A typical case involves reviewing the clients' health insurance plans, and then organizing and examining all the medical bills, insurance claims, and correspondence between patients, healthcare providers and facilities, and insurance companies. I [AGG] identify and contact the appropriate parties. Some of our other cases involved:

1. Providing key legislative contacts to a client who was tackling Medicare errors that had already cost him over $20,000 in legal fees to fight; on my recommendation, the client contacted the legislators to request additional fees be waived. The case was closed with no additional money required for the family to pay Medicare.
2. An insurance carrier repeatedly tried to deny a $17,000 hospital bill; I [AGG] intervened and succeeded in getting the denial overturned.
3. Helping an elderly woman's family fight a nursing home in New York City that is attempting to charge nearly double the top rate for skilled nursing care and is billing additional monthly fees that do not appear in any contract, I am working to get the facility to accept Medicare reimbursements; the case is now in the hands of the executive office of Medicare/Medicaid in New York City.

I frequently speak publicly to business and consumer groups about the current and upcoming health care laws, important insurance issues, and remind insured individuals that they are entitled to the insurance coverage they are paying for—and they have recourse when insurers don't want to pay for what is in the policy.

Many people have claimed bankruptcy because the health insurance carriers do not want to pay claims adequately. Our advice is to not give up, and fight for appropriate health insurance reimbursement.

6
Medicare Considerations

Avoid the Intense Pain When "Admitted to Hospital" Is Not What You Think

Have you heard of Medicare's two-midnight and three-midnight rules? These concern what Medicare Part A will cover for inpatient hospitalizations and overnight stays, and subsequent care in a skilled nursing facility.

Confusion, great upset and huge hospital bills occur when the patient was under the impression that he or she was admitted and treated on an inpatient basis (and therefore met the overnight-stay rules) when in fact, the hospital performed the procedure or administered treatment on an outpatient basis or the patient was kept under observation as an outpatient. In those cases, only doctors' services and outpatient services are covered by Medicare Part B, with associated deductibles and co-pays. Patients and their families must be vigilant and find out in advance how the hospital plans to categorize a stay to avoid unexpected emotional pain and financial turmoil.

The two- and three-midnight rules with Medicare have been problematic for people to understand and accept. Recently, there has been an increase in medical care expenses that are not reimbursed by Medicare. Further, when a Medicare patient leaves a hospital and is transferred to a rehabilitation or skilled nursing home, care in that facility will not be covered by Medicare Part A if the patient has not met the three-day inpatient stay requirement. This adds greatly to unexpected health care expenses.

In order to be covered by Part A (hospitalization and medication), the individual must stay in a hospital for two or more nights as an admitted patient on an inpatient basis. The three-night inpatient hospital rule is required if Medicare agrees to cover for a rehabilitation / skilled nursing home facility.

Speak with your doctor and have the doctor discuss it with the hospital billing department. It is the doctor's decision and the level of your condition that determine whether you are an inpatient. You need to fit the requirements first determined by your doctor and then agreed to by the hospital.

There are cases where someone is told he or she will be admitted, but it is not explained as to how. If not admitted as an inpatient, but only as an outpatient under observation, he or she will not be covered for Medicare Part A and rehab.

Coverage for Inpatient or Outpatient Procedures

Currently, hospitals are telling patients that they will be admitted to the hospital for the surgery or procedure. This is where the problem starts for many patients. What they do not know and are not being clearly told (until after entering the hospital and/or after the surgery or procedure is completed) is that, "they were admitted, but not admitted as an inpatient. They have been admitted as an **outpatient** (under observation)."

For example, a patient may go to the emergency room complaining of chest pains; the doctor sends the patient to the ICU for observation overnight. The condition resolves by the next morning and the patient goes home ... only to discover when the bill arrives, that this stay in the ICU is not covered as hospitalization by Medicare Part A; only the doctor's services are covered by Part B.

The Medicare website, http://www.medicare.gov/pubs/pdf/11435.pdf, states the following:

> You're an **inpatient** starting when you're formally admitted to a hospital with a doctor's order. The day **before** you're discharged is your last inpatient day.
>
> You're an **outpatient** if you're getting emergency department services, observation services, outpatient surgery, lab tests, X-rays, or any other hospital services, and the doctor **hasn't** written an order to admit you to a hospital as an inpatient. In these cases, you're an outpatient, even if you spend the night at the hospital.
>
> **Note:** Observation services are hospital outpatient services given to help the doctor decide if the patient needs to be admitted as an inpatient or can be discharged. Observation services may be given in the emergency department or another area of the hospital.

The decision for inpatient hospital admission is a complex medical decision based on your doctor's judgment and your need for medically necessary hospital care. An inpatient admission is generally appropriate when you're expected to need 2 or more midnights of medically necessary hospital care, but your doctor must order such admission, and the hospital must formally admit you in order for you to become an inpatient.

Currently, the hospital informs a patient that he or she is being admitted for surgery or a procedure. This is where the problem starts for many. What the patient may not know, and may not be clearly told until it's too late, is that they were not admitted as an inpatient, but as an outpatient (under observation). We have repeated this alert, as it is important.

This situation is not only confusing and upsetting; it has major ramifications for Medicare coverage. As an outpatient, the patient must pay for:

1. Hospital room and board.
2. Medications.
3. Rehabilitation/skilled nursing fees if he or she goes to a rehab facility after leaving the hospital. Rehabilitation daily fees often range between $400 and $800 a day, not including additional fees for physical therapy, speech therapy and/or occupational therapy.

What You Can Do

This lack of transparency on the part of hospitals is unsettling, to say the least. What can be done about it?

Hospitals must put clear communication with patients about their admission status and Medicare coverage at the top of any treatment plan. Patients and their families must be aware of the potential for confusion about how they are being admitted—"inpatient admittance" or "outpatient admittance"—and ask questions of their physicians or hospitals either before or upon being admitted to the hospital. Find out how the hospital plans to categorize your stay, and whether subsequent sub-acute care will be covered and if the three-night minimum inpatient stay is being met.

It is difficult enough having to go through medical procedures or surgeries; there is no reason to compound the situation by discovering that Medicare won't cover hospital stays or rehabilitative treatment because of inpatient vs. outpatient status.

7
Medicare Appeals Information

This chapter will outline the Medicare appeals procedures, first from the Internet site medicare.gov, and then from the Official U.S. Government Medicare Handbook, *Medicare & You*. Naturally, they boil down to much the same things.

Medicare.gov, "The Official U.S. Government Site for Medicare"

Information on filing an appeal if you "disagree with a coverage or payment decision made by Medicare, your Medicare health plan, or your Medicare Prescription Drug Plan" can be obtained at the following Internet link:

- http://www.medicare.gov/claims-and-appeals/file-an-appeal/appeals.html

This was the first link obtained when using Google to search on "Medicare Appeals." You can also reach this site by starting at http://www.medicare.gov.

You can appeal to try to get a denial reversed for:

1. a request for health care services, supply, item, or prescription drug;

2. a request for payment for a health care service, supply, item, or prescription drug;
3. a request to change the amount your must pay for a health care service, supply, item, or prescription drug;
4. stoppage by your plan of providing or paying for all or part of a health care service, supply, item, or prescription drug.

If you decide to appeal, "ask your doctor, health care provider, or supplier for any information that may help your case. See your plan materials or contact your plan for details about your appeal rights."

"The appeals process has 5 levels. If you disagree with the decision made at any level of the process, you can generally go on to the next level. At each level, you'll be given instructions in the decision letter on how to move to the next level of appeal."

This site page then lists more links to obtaining information on the following:

- Original Medicare appeals
- Medicare health plan appeals
- Medicare prescription drug coverage appeals
- Special Needs Plan appeals
- Get help filing an appeal.

Official U.S. Government Medicare Handbook, *Medicare & You.*

This is based on the 2015 Edition, pp. 120-125.

You can appeal to try to get a denial reversed for:

1. a request for health care services, supply, item, or prescription drug;
2. a request for payment for a health care service, supply, item, or prescription drug;

3. a request to change the amount your must pay for a health care service, supply, item, or prescription drug;
4. stoppage by your plan of providing or paying for all or part of a health care service, supply, item, or prescription drug.

If you decide to appeal, "ask your doctor, health care provider, or supplier for any information that may help your case. Keep a copy of everything you send to Medicare or your plan as part of your appeal."

"How you file an appeal depends on the type of Medicare coverage you have:

If You Have Original Medicare
1. Get the 'Medicare Summary Notice' (MSN) that shows the item or service that you are appealing....
2. Circle the item(s) you disagree with on the MSN, and write an explanation of why you disagree....
3. Include your name, phone number and Medicare number on the MSN, and sign it. Keep a copy for your records.
4. Send the MSN, or a copy, to the company that handles bills for Medicare listed on the MSN....
5. You must file the appeal within 120 days of the date you get the MSN in the mail."

See the handbook for the details left out by the ellipses [....].

If You Have a Medicare Health Plan
Learn how to file an appeal by looking at the materials your plan sends you, calling your plan, or visiting Medicare.gov/appeals."

If You Have a Medicare Prescription Drug Plan
You have the right to do all these (even before you buy a certain drug):

1. Get a written explanation (called a "coverage determination")….
2. Ask for an exception: if needed drug isn't in the plan's formulary, if a coverage rule should be waived, if you cannot take a less expensive drug for your condition.

"You or your prescriber must contact your plan to ask for a coverage determination or an exception…." Similarly, make requests for benefits you haven't received yet, payment for drugs already bought, expedited service, explanations.

If you think your services are ending too soon, you can ask for a fast appeal, an "expedited determination." This handbook contains more details on this and the other topics on this chapter.

Advanced Beneficiary Notice of Noncoverage (ABN)

Your provider may give you an ABN if it thinks Medicare will not cover this. If you still go ahead with the service, you are agreeing to pay if Medicare does not. Have your provider apply to Medicare for payment, if you wish, and you may get it paid or may start an appeal.

Nursing facilities and equipment and supplies providers may also issue ABNs.

Note: "If your provider was required to give you an ABN but didn't, in most cases your provider must pay you back what you paid for this item or service."

8
Affordable Care Act ["Obama Care"] Appeals

This material is from the Department of Health and Human Services web site:

- http://www.hhs.gov/healthcare/rights/appeal/appealing-health-plan-decisions.html

Appealing Health Plan Decisions

Under the Affordable Care Act, you have the right to appeal a health insurance company's decision to deny payment for a claim or to terminate your health coverage. The following rules for appeals apply to health plans created after March 23, 2010, and to older plans that have been changed in certain ways since that date.

You can appeal your insurance company's decision through an "internal appeal," in which you ask your insurance company to do a full and fair review of its decision. If your insurance company still denies payment or coverage, the law permits you to have an independent third party decide to uphold or overturn the plan's decision. This final process is often referred to as an "external review."

Your state may have a Consumer Assistance Program that can help you file an appeal or request a review of your health insurance company's decision if you are not sure what steps to take. Your insurance company should have provided you with information about how to file an appeal and the appeals process when you were enrolled in coverage, and there may be information about the process on the plan's website. Visit LocalHelp.HealthCare.gov to find help in your area.

Internal Appeals

Your internal appeals rights take effect when your plan starts a new plan year or policy year on or after September 23, 2010. Learn more here about internal appeals (appeals made through your insurance company).

External Review

If after an internal appeal the plan still denies your request for payment or services, you can ask for an independent external review. For plan years or policy years that begin on or after July 1, 2011, your plan must include information on your denial notice about how to request this review. If your state has a Consumer Assistance Program, that program can help you with this request. If the external reviewer reverses your insurance company's denial, your insurance company must give you the payments or services you requested in your claim.

What This Means for You

If your insurance company denies payment for a claim or terminates your health coverage, you can request an appeal. When your insurance company receives your request, it is required to review and explain its decision. The insurance company must also let you know how you can disagree with its decision. It is required to start and complete the process in a timely manner.

If you don't speak English, you may be entitled to receive appeals information in the language you speak upon request (Spanish and some other languages are available). This right applies to plan years or policy years that started on or after January 1, 2012.

Some Important Details

Health plans that started on or before March 23, 2010, may be "grandfathered health plans." The appeals and review rights don't apply to them.

Appeal rights depend on the state you live in and the type of health plan you have. Some group plans may require more than one level of internal appeal before you can request an external review.

For More Information

If you have questions about internal appeals and external reviews, call your health plan or state insurance regulator.

Find detailed technical and regulatory information on appealing health plan decisions.

Learn about other consumer protections in the health care law.

Content created by Assist. Sec./Public Affairs - Digital Communications Division. Content last reviewed on September 16, 2014.

Under the Affordable Care Act, ACA, if you purchased insurance through the state, then most of the time, you are not allowed to go out of state for medical services.

9
Out-of-Network Protection Legislation

On April 4, 2015, Caroline Chen of Bloomberg News reported:

> "Hospital patients in New York are the latest in the nation to gain legal protection against unexpected bills from doctors who won't accept their insurance.
>
> "New York this week extended patient protections to restrict out-of-network providers from 'balance-billing' customers for emergency care or when patients can't choose their doctors. Balance-billling occurs when health workers who don't accept a patient's insurance try to collect the difference between their charge and the insurer's reimbursement."

Chen cited a Kaiser Family Foundation statement that New York is one of 13 states with such laws. A Foundation spokesperson, Karen Pollitz, is quoted as noting, "It's a pretty good bet that if you're hospitalized or having any kind of surgery, somebody along the way who touches you or your slides or films will not be in network." That can lead to major unreimbursed expenses. Ms. Chen's article gives just such an example of high, unreimbursed costs.

Generally, claims are negotiable for out-of-network providers.
A new consumer protection law went into effect on April 1

in New York—the **Emergency Medical Services and Surprise Bills Law**—which protects patients from unexpected expenses related to out-of-network and emergency medical services. The legislation creates more transparency by requiring more disclosure of how much patients can expect to pay for medical care and about providers' and facilities' health plan participation.

What's a Surprise Bill?

Patients have been surprised plenty in the past by unexpected medical bills and unreimbursed expenses. According to the New York State Department of Financial Services, **surprise bills occur when services a) are performed by a non-participating (out-of-network) doctor at a participating hospital or ambulatory surgical center in the patient's HMO or insurer's network or b) when a participating doctor refers an insured to a non-participating provider.** The new law also protects all consumers from bills for emergency services. Full details about surprise bills, how to avoid them and how to dispute them are available at **http://www.dfs.ny.gov/consumer/hprotection.htm**

The new law aims to eradicate these unexpected charges that arise in certain situations such as:

1. **Services rendered by a non-participating physician at a participating hospital or ambulatory surgical center.** Situations include when a participating physician is unavailable, a non-participating physician renders services without the insured's knowledge, or unforeseen medical services arise at the time the health care services are rendered. It is *not* a surprise bill if you chose to receive services from a non-participating doctor instead of from an available participating doctor.
2. **Services rendered by a non-participating provider without explicit acknowledgment and consent from the insured.** In this case, the services were referred by a participating

physician to a non-participating provider; the insured patient did not give explicit written consent acknowledging this referral and the referral results in costs not covered by the health care plan.
3. **Uninsured for services**. A patient who is not insured for services rendered by a physician at a hospital or ambulatory surgical center has not received all the disclosures required pursuant to Section 24 of the public health law in a timely manner.

Several provisions of the law affect health insurance plans:*

All health plans must hold patients harmless for emergency services (except for in-network cost-share). In essence, all emergency services must be treated as in-network care.

Plans that offer out-of-network coverage must make available one product that bases reimbursement on the "usual and customary" rate.

The law requires disclosure for non-emergency services from health plans, physicians, health care professionals, and hospitals.

Establishes an independent entity to resolve disputes over physician fees and plan reimbursement for emergency and "surprise bills."

*Source: Healthcare Association of New York State (www.hayns.org)

New Disclosures Help Avoid Financial Distress

Hospitals and health care providers must include a lot of new information on their websites so the public has easy access to these disclosures.

For hospitals/facilities these include health plan participation, statements that in-hospital physician services are not included in hospital charges (a common point of confusion), that physicians/

providers might not participate in the same plans as the hospital (another confusing issue), and an advisory to determine the practitioner's plan participation in advance. Hospitals must post the contact information of the physician groups they contract with and instructions on how to contact them.

Medical providers must clearly state:

1. the names of their participating health plans (in writing or on the provider's website and verbally when an appointment is scheduled);
2. the names of the physician's hospital affiliations (same manner as above);
3. for non-emergency services, that the amount or estimated amount for the service is available upon request; and
4. upon receipt of a request, the amount or estimated amount that will be billed—excepting any unforeseen medical circumstances that may arise when the services are provided (this information must be disclosed in writing);
5. the name, practice name, address, and phone number of any provider scheduled to perform anesthesiology, laboratory, pathology, radiology, or assistant surgeon services
    a. in connection with care provided in the physician's office or
    b. referred or coordinated by the physician for the patient;
6. similarly, for patients scheduled either for hospital admission or outpatient hospital service, the name, practice name, address, and phone number of any other physician whose services will be arranged by the physician and are scheduled at the time of the pre-admission testing, registration, or admission [or] at the time that the non-emergency services are scheduled;
7. additionally, information as to how to determine the healthcare

plans in which the physician participates, and how to determine this in a timely manner.

There are many more stipulations now in place to protect New York consumers from unforeseen medical expenses. Anyone who receives a surprise bill for health care services and wants the services to be treated as in-network, can fill out a New York State Out-of-Network Surprise Medical Bill Assignment of Benefits Form to dispute certain denied out-of-network or emergency care reimbursements. You can also work with an independent medical insurance advocate to resolve insurance issues on your behalf and recoup medical reimbursements you are entitled to, according to your health plan and the law.

10

Medicare Supplement (Medigap) Plans

Medigap is the supplemental coverage after Medicare: Medicare covers 80%, Medigap 20%.

Medigap plans are offered by private insurance companies. As shown below, there is a standardized set of plan options. These are **also called "Medicare Supplemental Insurance"** and are in most states identified by letters. These are described briefly here, and then the appeals and grievance procedures are outlined for one of the major private plans, United Healthcare, offered through AARP, the Medigap plan one of the authors [DWC] now has.

The Medigap policy covers coinsurance only after you've paid the deductible (unless the Medigap policy also pays the deductible).

Compare Medigap Plans Side-by-Side

The chart below shows basic information about the different benefits the Medigap policies cover.

Key:

Y = the plan covers 100% of this benefit
N = the policy doesn't cover that benefit
% = the plan covers that percentage of this benefit
+ = N/A = not applicable

Medigap Benefits						Medigap Plans				
	A	B	C	D	F*	G	K	L	M	N
Part A coinsurance and hospital costs up to an additional 365 days after Medicare benefits used up	Y	Y	Y	Y	Y	Y	Y	Y	Y	Y
Part B coinsurance or copayment	Y	Y	Y	Y	Y	Y	50%	75%	Y	Y***
Blood (first 3 pints)	Y	Y	Y	Y	Y	Y	50%	75%	Y	Y
Part A hospice care coinsurance or copayment	Y	Y	Y	Y	Y	Y	50%	75%	Y	Y
Skilled nursing facility care coinsurance	N	N	Y	Y	Y	Y	50%	75%	Y	Y
Part A deductible	N	Y	Y	Y	Y	Y	50%	75%	50%	Y
Part B deductible	N	N	Y	N	Y	N	N	N	N	N
Part B excess charges	N	N	N	N	Y	Y	N	N	N	N
Foreign travel exchange (up to plan limits)	N	N	80%	80%	80%	80%	N	N	80%	80%
Out-of-pocket limit**	+	+	+	+	+	+	$4,940	$2,470	+	+

* Plan F also offers a high-deductible plan. If you choose this option, this means you must pay for Medicare-covered costs up to the deductible amount of $2,180 in 2015 before your Medigap plan pays anything.
** After you meet your out-of-pocket yearly limit and your yearly Part B deductible, the Medigap plan pays 100% of covered services for the rest of the calendar year.
*** Plan N pays 100% of the Part B coinsurance, except for a

copayment of up to $20 for some office visits and up to a $50 copayment for emergency room visits that don't result in inpatient admission.

If you live in Massachusetts, Minnesota, or Wisconsin, Medigap policies are standardized in a different way. For more information;

1. find a Medigap policy and inquire at its provider,
2. call your State Health Insurance Assistance Program (SHIP),
3. call your State Insurance Department

Based on Medicare.gov, a federal government website managed by the Centers for Medicare & Medicaid Services, 7500 Security Boulevard, Baltimore, MD 21244

United Healthcare Medigap Appeals and Grievances Process

This is based on the United Healthcare website www.unitedhealthcaresolutons.com.

Coverage decisions and appeals: This "deals with problems related to your benefits and coverage for medical services and prescription drugs, including problems related to payment."

Asking for coverage decisions: Determining whether or not to pay and how much to pay for your medical services or drugs is a "coverage decision," and if you disagree, you can make an appeal.

Members can appeal or have representatives appeal for them.

When appeals can be filed: "within sixty (60) calendar days of the date of the notice of the initial organization determination." You can appeal refusals to pay, refusals to provide service, reductions or stopping of service.

Details are supplied for where to file the appeal and what to include.

What happens next: "If you appeal, UnitedHealthcare will review the decision. If any of the services you requested is still denied after our review, Medicare will provide you with a new and impartial review of your case by a reviewer outside of our Medicare Advantage Organization or prescription drug plan. If you disagree with that decision, you will have further appeal rights...."

Fast decision/expedited appeals: "You have the right to request and receive expedited decisions affecting your medical treatment in 'Time-Sensitive' situations...." Details are supplied.

Member Grievances

"A grievance is a type of complaint you make if you have a complaint or problem that does not involve payment or services by your Medicare Advantage health plan or a Contracting Medical Provider." Examples given are: poor care, long waiting times, being unable to get the information you need, unsanitary conditions in a doctor's office, and instances of problems caused by misinformation, misunderstanding, lack of information.

Grievances should be filed within sixty (60) days of the circumstances giving rise to the grievance.

They should be filed by calling UnitedHealthcare Customer Service, 8 a.m. to 8 p.m., local time, seven days a week.

11
Medicare Advantage Plans

Somewhat different from the Medigap plans are the Medicare Advantage Plans. Medicare Advantage Plans are not free lunches. They have deductibles and many have large co-pays. They are said to undermine regular Medicare with the big deductibles and to subsidize insurance companies who contract the Medicare Advantage Plans.

AARP offers an advantage plan – United HealthCare. The following website from Medicare describes the difference between a Medigap Plan and a Medicare Advantage Plan:

- http://www.aarp.org/health/medicare-insurance/info-09-2010/ask_ms_medicare__question_87.html

When you look at the next website, you will see three options for Advantage plans through AARP United Healthcare Medicare: HMO, POS, and PPO:

- https://www.aarpmedicareplans.com/health-plans/medicare-advantage-plans.html

The PPO is only one that does not require possible referrals. The PPO would be the best when it comes to doctors, but who knows

how much your out-of-pocket expenses will be? For example: currently, half of the doctors at New York's Hospital for Special Surgery and Hospital for Joint Diseases do not take any health insurance – **half of the best doctors out there are no longer taking any insurance.**
Notes:

1. When someone is on an Advantage plan, they cannot be covered by any other insurance.
2. When they have Medicare with a supplemental plan, they can have additional coverage, even unlimited.

Blue Cross / Blue Shield (BC/BS) Medicare provides a detailed chart at the following site:

- http://www.bcbs.com/already-a-member/the-blues-and-medicare/medicare-advantage-state-listing.html

This indicates BC/BS has Medicare Advantage Plans in different states. In the NY area BC/BS offers Local PPO and HMO.

Below again is the link for the HMO Blue Cross / Blue Shield Plan for a Medicare Advantage Plan:

- https://www.empireblue.com/shop/content/olspublic/pdf/2015/english/HMO_Kit_Sel_Put_NY.pdf

Availability of this plan in New York State, for example, varies county-by-county, so this plan is not available in Orange County, NY ---only neighboring Putnam, Rockland and Westchester.

On this policy you have limited coverage, only HMO doctors –- HMO doctors are the only BC/BS doctors that are on the plan. The good thing is that you have a monthly premium of $69 (quite reasonable --- the government pays the difference), the deductible for prescription drugs is $273, the yearly limit out of pocket is $6,700 for services you have for in-network doctors. The disadvantage is that you are not covered for out-of-network providers. If you have expenses that are out-of-network, those expenses are not counted towards your $6,700 limit, which can be costly. If the medication is not on their plan, you will be paying out of pocket. The mental health plan and out-patient rehab are very limited. If you need renal care you are only covered at 20%.

If you are very sick and expect to be in and out of hospitals multiple times of the year, it seems best to have Medicare with a supplementary insurance coverage and to be sure that the Medicare Supplemental plan, a Medigap plan, is the best offered.

If you are not likely to be sick, then the Medicare Advantage plan will cost less and will be quite financially beneficial.

The following website from Medicare summarizes the differences between a Medigap Plan and a Medicare Advantage Plan:

- http://www.aarp.org/health/medicare-insurance/info-09-2010/ask_ms_medicare__question_87.html

12
Catastrophic Coverage Plans

This is a summary. For more information on catastrophic plans, please see:

- https://www.healthcare.gov/choose-a-plan/catastrophic-plans/

If you are under 30 or qualify for the below-listed hardships, you are eligible for a catastrophic plan. This is what information is available on the website, which is extremely limited unless you fill out a marketplace application:

People under 30 and people with "hardship exemptions" may buy a "catastrophic" health plan. This type of plan has lower monthly premiums and mainly protects you from very high medical costs.

Protection from Worst-case Scenarios

A catastrophic plan generally requires you to pay all of your medical costs up to a certain amount, usually several thousand dollars. This limit is known as a "deductible." After you reach your deductible, the costs for essential health benefits are generally paid by the catastrophic plan.

Catastrophic plans usually have lower monthly premiums than a comprehensive plan. They cover your costs only after you've used a lot of care, protecting you from worst-case financial scenarios like serious accidents or illnesses.

Catastrophic plans cover prevention and some primary care.

In the Marketplace, catastrophic plans cover three primary care visits per year at no cost, even before you've met your deductible. They also cover free preventive services.

If you buy a catastrophic plan in the Marketplace, you can't get premium tax credits or lower out-of-pocket costs based on your income. **Regardless of your income, you pay the standard price for the catastrophic plan.**

Catastrophic Plans with a Hardship Exemption

People 30 years of age and older, with a "hardship exemption" may buy a catastrophic plan. Hardship exemptions from paying the fee are granted to people based on income or other factors that prevent them from getting coverage.

If you had an individual insurance plan that was cancelled and you believe other Marketplace plans aren't affordable, you may qualify for a hardship exemption. If you do, you can buy a catastrophic plan.

After you fill out a Marketplace application, you'll get an eligibility notice. It will tell you what programs and savings you're eligible for, including catastrophic plans. If you're eligible to enroll in a catastrophic plan, you'll see these plans listed when you compare your coverage options.

You can then choose to enroll in a catastrophic plan or any other plan available to you.

The Hardship Exemptions

Hardships that qualify you for exemptions include:

1. You were homeless.
2. You were evicted in the past 6 months or were facing eviction or foreclosure.

3. You received a shut-off notice from a utility company.
4. You recently experienced domestic violence.
5. You recently experienced the death of a close family member.
6. You experienced a fire, flood, or other natural or human-caused disaster that caused substantial damage to your property.
7. You filed for bankruptcy in the last 6 months.
8. You had medical expenses you couldn't pay in the last 24 months that resulted in substantial debt.
9. You experienced unexpected increases in necessary expenses due to caring for an ill, disabled, or aging family member.
10. You expect to claim a child as a tax dependent who's been denied coverage in Medicaid and CHIP, and another person is required by court order to give medical support to the child. In this case, you don't have the pay the penalty for the child.
11. As a result of an eligibility appeals decision, you're eligible for enrollment in a qualified health plan (QHP) through the Marketplace, lower costs on your monthly premiums, or cost-sharing reductions for a time period when you weren't enrolled in a QHP through the Marketplace.
12. You were determined ineligible for Medicaid because your state didn't expand eligibility for Medicaid under the Affordable Care Act.
13. Your individual insurance plan was cancelled, and you believe other Marketplace plans are unaffordable.
14. You experienced another hardship in obtaining health insurance.

13

Patient Information Resources

As part of its commitment to the public, MedWise Insurance Advocacy provides this list of resources having valuable information about medical billing, the healthcare industry, and New York State and nationwide healthcare-insurance-related web links.

These resources include information about Medicaid and Medicare along with MedWise Insurance Advocacy's business affiliations.

Allergy & Asthma Network Mothers of Asthmatics
www.allergyhome.org/blogger/allergy-asthma-network-mothers-of-asthmatics-aanma-and-our-community/
or
www.allergyhome.org/blogger/

Alliance to End Childhood Lead Poisoning
www.nchh.org/Portals/0/Contents/Another_Link_in_Chain.pdf

Alzheimer's Association
www.alz.org

Alzheimer's Foundation
www.alzfdn.org

Alzheimer's Speaks
www.alzheimersspeaks.com

American Association of Homes and Services for the Aging
www.retirement-living.com/proaging-network/american-association-of-homes-and-services-for-the-aging-aahsa-officially-becomes-leadingage/
or
www.levinassociates.com/company/leading-age

American Association of Retired Persons
www.aarp.org/

American Autoimmune Related Diseases Association
www.aarda.org/

American Cancer Society
www.cancer.org/

American College of Preventive Medicine
www.acpm.org/

American Heart Association
www.heart.org/

American Lung Association
www.lung.org/

American Medical Association
ama-assn.org/

American Psychiatric Foundation Americans with Disabilities Act
www.usccr.gov/pubs/ada/ch5.htm
or
www.apa.org/pi/disability/resources/publications/ada.aspx

American Psychological Association
www.apa.org/

American Public Health Association
www.apha.org/

Arthritis Foundation
www.arthritis.org/

Association of Maternal and Child Health Programs
www.amchp.org/

Association of Public Health Laboratories
www.aphl.org/

Association of State and Territorial Health Officials
www.astho.org/

Asthma and Allergy Foundation of America
www.aafa.org/

Autism Society of America
www.autism-society.org/

Autism Speaks
www.autismspeaks.org/

Beyond Pesticides/National Coalition Against the Misuse of Pesticides
www.earthshare.org/2009/09/beyond-pesticid.html
or
www.beyondpesticides.org/

The Breast Cancer Fund
www.breastcancerfund.org/

Centers for Medicare & Medicaid Services
www.cms.gov/

Center for Science in the Public Interest
www.cspinet.org/

Children of Aging Parents
www.agingcare.com/adult-children-aging-parents
or
www.acapcommunity.com/

Children's Environmental Health Network
www.cehn.org/

Children's Health Environmental Coalition
www.cehn.org/childrens_health_environmental_coalition
or
www.consumer-action.org/hcop/articles/
the_childrens_health_environmental_coalition

Coalition for Children's Health
www.healthychildrencoalition.org/

Council of State and Territorial Epidemiologists
www.cste.org/

Department of Health and Human Services
www.hhs.gov/

Disability.gov
eMedNY System
www.emedny.org/

Epilepsy Foundation of America
www.epilepsy.com/

FRAXA Research Foundation
www.fraxa.org/

HIPAA
www.hhs.gov/ocr/privacy/
or
www.hhs.gov/ocr/privacy/hipaa/understanding/

Joint Council of Asthma, Allergy & Immunology
www.jcaai.org/
or
www.aaaai.org/

Juvenile Diabetes Research Foundation
jdrf.org/

March of Dimes Foundation
www.marchofdimes.org/

Medicaid
medicaid.gov/

Medicare
www.medicare.gov/

National Association of County and City Health Officials
www.naccho.org

National Association of School Nurses
www.nasn.org/

National Clearinghouse for Alcohol and Drug Information
ncadd.org/
or
healthliteracy.worlded.org/docs/culture/materials/orgs_015.html

National Government Services
www.ngsservices.com/
or
www.ngsmedicare.com/

National Institute of Mental Health (NIMH)
www.nimh.nih.gov/

National Institutes of Health National Organization for Rare Disorders (NORD)
www.rarediseases.org/
or
www.rarediseases.org/

National Plan and Provider Enumeration System
nppes.cms.hhs.gov/NPPES/Welcome.do

New England Journal of Medicine
www.nejm.org/

NHIC, Corp.
www.medicarenhic.com/

Pancreatic Cancer Action Network
https://www.pancan.org/

Partnership for Prevention
www.prevent.org/

Physicians for Social Responsibility
www.psr.org/

Research! America
www.researchamerica.org/

RxList
www.rxlist.com/

Sarcoidosis Awareness Network
www.sarcoidosisnetwork.net/
or
www.sarcoid-network.org/

The National Institute on Aging
www.nia.nih.gov/

Tourette Syndrome Association
www.tsa-usa.org/

Trust for America's Health
healthyamericans.org/

United Cerebral Palsy Association
ucp.org/

U.S. Department of Justice
www.justice.gov/

U.S. House of Representatives
www.house.gov/

United State Senate
www.senate.gov/

APPENDIX 1
About MedWise Insurance Advocacy

Regardless of how good your health insurance plan is, you are bound to bump up against issues regarding payments for services you thought were covered, overpayments, wrongful billing, and denied medical claims at least once in your life.

Many baby boomers are also confronting their aging parents' mounting medical needs, healthcare costs, and navigating the murky waters of Medicare, Medicaid, secondary insurers, and unattended medical bills. Depending on their age, they could also be dealing with these issues for themselves.

Working with a medical insurance advocate can relieve a lot of this burden, and provide much-needed support to individuals and families who are fighting with their health insurance carriers or healthcare providers over medical bills and claims—or simply need help wading through, organizing, and prioritizing a growing mountain of them. Even if you are well, as a busy entrepreneur or business owner, your mind is on other matters related to your business—not on figuring out if you paid too much, if your coverage is right, or if that denied medical claim has merit.

What a Medical Insurance Advocate Does

Let's face it: when someone is dealing with an illness or recovering from surgery, and those bills start flowing in from multiple physicians, hospitals, and rehab centers, it doesn't take long for the situation to become overwhelming and confusing. Sorting through the Explanations of Benefits and trying to understand exactly what is covered and what is not—often revealed once those unexpected charges come through—can become a burden very quickly.

Insurance advocates act as the expert liaisons between patients and providers. They work with patients regarding their health insurance coverage, medical bills and claims, and can handle all communication and paperwork with the insurance carriers as well as medical facilities or service providers. They are the bridge between patients and health insurance companies, acting on their clients' behalf to get claims passed, to ensure the highest coverage allowed (depending on the health plan), and to enable patients and their families to rest easy knowing their insurance matters are in expert hands.

Many medical insurance advocates also work with elder law and personal injury attorneys to make sure that all their clients' medical claims are processed and paid correctly.

These experienced professionals sort through and resolve clients' medical bills, lien claims, insurance pre-authorizations, denied medical claims, and medical letters of appeal. They can explain those bewildering Explanations of Benefits and advocate for patients regarding any insurance issues that require expert or objective attention.

Below is a summary of savings obtained for their clients by MedWise:

MedWise Cases: Savings		
Client's City	Service Year	Savings
Las Vegas, NV	2012	$36,000
Kingston, PA	2012	$19,000
Great River, NY	2013	$8,858
Staten Island, NY	2012	$36,075
Monroe, NY	2014	$75,000
Mamaroneck, NY	2014	$10,000
Onsted, MI	2013	$75,000
New Milford, NJ		$21,000
Hartsdale, NY	2014	$10,000
Englewood, NJ	2014	$50,000
Blooming Grove, NY	2009	$10,000
Newburgh, NY	2009	$1,300
New Windsor, NY		$8,700
Washington Crossing, PA	2011	$45,000
Brooklyn, NY		$20,000
New York, NY	2011	$37,267
Nanuet, NY		$41,000
Bronxville, NY	2011	$3,091
Croton-on-Hudson, NY	2012	$2,000
Saco, ME	2007	$84,000
Astoria, NY	2012	$24,800
Woodmere, NY	2011	$9,835
New Windsor, NY		$5 000
Middleburgh, NY	1995	$1,400
Beverly Hills, CA	2005	$10,800
Greer, SC	2013	$36,901
Goshen, NY	2014	$12,000
NJ		$100,000
NY		$175,000
Nanuet, NY		$885,000
TN		$6,158

MedWise Cases: Savings		
Client's City	Service Year	Savings
Hampton Bays, NY	2013	$4,100
Golden's Bridge, NY	2013	$30,000
Westfield, NJ	2014	$35,623
Westfield, NJ		$176,000
Clinton, NJ		$3,630
New York, NY	2014	$1,500
Wilmington, DE		$15,000
Hollis Hills, NY	2014	$20,067
Port Jervis, NY	2011	$11,503
Pleasantville, NY	2014	$225,000
Newburgh, NY	2009	$1,052
Brooklyn, NY	2013	$66,340
Katonah, NY	2013	$3,126
Chicago, IL	2013	$3,126
Huntington Station, NY		$10,000
White Haven, PA		$17,000
Spring Valley, NY		$10,000
New York, NY	2013	$50,000
Queens Village, NY	2011	$100,000
Atlanta, GA	2013	$35,000
Houston, TX	2014	$100,000
Monroe, NY	2011	$360
Lincoln Park, NJ	2014	$18,000
Jackson Hills, NY	2012	$2,260
Seymour, CT		$27,000
Annandale, NJ	2012	$15,408
Arlington, TN	2014	$22,346
San Clemente, CA		$59,600
New York, NY		$58,932
New York, NY		$10,000
Passaic, NJ	2015	$300,000

MedWise Cases: Savings		
Client's City	**Service Year**	**Savings**
New York, NY		$3,000
New Windsor, NY		$10,000
Conroe, TX		$3,700
Brooklyn, NY		$3,000
Clifton, NJ	2014	$1,200
Los Angeles, CA		$13,390
Lebanon, NJ		$3,142
New York, NY	2012	$37,057
New Windsor, NY		$1,099
Margate, NJ	2014	$90,000
Mandeville, LA	2012	$16,021
NY	2015	$18,000
Rye, NY	2015	$600,000
Warren, NJ	2010	$25,000
The Woodlands, TX	2014	$200,000
New York, NY	2014	$1,000
Nanuet, NY		$135,803
White Plains, NY	2006	$50,000
Albany, NY		$16,937
Hillsborough, NJ	2014	$15,000
New York, NY	2014	$15,000
Milford, PA	2011	$12,100
Shaker Heights, OH	2014	$2,922
College Point, NY	2014	$900
Armonk, NY	2010	$3,000
New York, NY	2013	$239,157

APPENDIX 2
Award Nominations for Adria Goldman Gross

I highly recommend Ms. Adria Gross for the *Westchester Magazine's* "Healthcare Heroes" award. She is a true and passionate advocate for individuals facing major health insurance challenges and works tirelessly on behalf of her clients, many of whom reside in Westchester County. She is also a community leader and a supporter of a number of not-for-profit groups.

Adria has been honored for her work on behalf of her clients, including being named by New York's WCBS Newsradio 880 as one of their "Women of Achievement" in 2013. Also in 2013, due to efforts to start a YWCA in her home county, she received a YWCA Special Award in Appreciation for Spirit, Drive and Dedication for Bringing a Y Presence to Southern Orange County, New York. She is currently a member of the Central Westchester Geriatric Committee and has been very involved in programs sponsored by Westchester County's Department of Senior Programs and Services.

With her background in the insurance industry, Adria brings to her work a depth of knowledge that few others have. She started her own business, MedWise Billing, Inc., in 2007, and, in spite of her own health issues, has grown that business and helped many clients who have been overwhelmed by their health care issues. A number of them have left glowing testimonials on her website. She is considered to be someone who has great strength of character and who brings empathy and concern to her clients' needs. She does not give up and truly goes the extra mile for her clients. Her colleagues also attest to her integrity and the support she provides to them when they call upon her for help.

As an elder law attorney in Westchester County who has come to know Adria and admire her dedication to her clients, her enthusiasm for her work and her depth of knowledge, I believe that Adria is a true "Healthcare Hero" and deserving of Westchester Magazine's "Healthcare Heroes" award.

Betsy Klempert

It is my pleasure to write a letter of recommendation for Adria Gross to participate in Leadership Rockland. Adria would be a great addition to Leadership Rockland and has much to offer the community. She has been an outstanding community leader with significant accomplishments and is poised to take an increasing role in the vital healthcare debate.

One of the things I admire so much about Adria is how she overcame so much adversity in her life. For many years she was plagued by epileptic seizures. She has surmounted this challenge of her youth and young adulthood so completely that one would never have an inkling unless she mentions this. One outcome of this adversity is that Adria has an unusual degree of empathy and has gone to great lengths to help disabled people. Among other awards, she was named Volunteer of the Year by the Autism Group of Orange County.

Professionally, Adria is an expert in medical billing issues and the healthcare system. She is a dynamic speaker and has appeared frequently in the media including nationally televised news programs on CBS and elsewhere. Her energy and diligence are well known in the community.

With health issues so critical to the nation and especially pressing in Rockland, Adria is an important asset to the community. While Adria lives in Monroe, she has been active in the business community and nonprofits in Rockland for many years and plans to increase that involvement. Participating in Leadership Rockland is a logical next step for her and would greatly benefit the Rockland community.

Regards,
Larry Luxenberg
Lexington Avenue Capital Management

It is my pleasure to recommend Ms. Adria Gross for Leadership Rockland.

This is a personal reference; hence I am not using the Letterhead of ARC of Rockland, where I am employed as the Deputy Executive Director of the not-for-profit agency.

I have had a personal relationship with Ms. Gross for many years. She lives in my neighborhood, attends the same gym and house of worship, and we communicate on a regular basis. You could say that I am one of her most ardent supporters.

Rarely have I come across an individual with such an outstanding reservoir of knowledge, and yet, an enthusiasm to learn. Every endeavor she pursues, she demonstrates her caring for the people she is working with, her quest for reaching satisfactory outcomes, and her dedication to perfection.

What is remarkable is that she routinely surmounts every obstacle, both personal and professional, thrown her way.

Because I have lived in Orange County and have worked in Rockland for over 30 years, I know that Leadership Rockland will play a significant role in connecting Ms. Gross to the people she needs to interact with. Through my work, I have seen many individuals succeed following their experience in Leadership Rockland, and believe she will do the same.

Please do not hesitate to contact me if you have any questions.

Sincerely,
Steven J. Rubinsky, Ph.D.

I have known Adria Gross for the past five years. In that time, I have been amazed at how dedicated a person she is. She has great perseverance which is required when trying to get money for her clients from the insurance companies. She surveys every avenue available to her that she knows and keeps questioning and learning more and more about new possibilities to try. This is what makes her so good at being an advocate for others. Also, Adria tackles every new job with a dedication to getting it done well and timely. This is not always true in business situations. She is compassionate, easy to talk to, values confidentiality and is professional in every way. I value working with her and also being called her friend.

Sincerely yours,
Eugene Price, CPA

My family had the good fortune to find Adria Gross and her company MedWise Insurance Advocacy during a very traumatic period in our lives. My late father, who was in the process of immigrating into the United States due to his advanced age, suffered a series of hospitalizations before he became eligible for affordable comprehensive health insurance. Quickly, we found ourselves struggling with enormous medical bills, confusing insurance denials, and a growing pile of threatening letters from collection agencies. We desperately needed help and started searching for a healthcare advocate. After interviewing several consultants, we found Adria. That is when things started to get better.

We were immediately comforted by Adria's high level of concern and empathy, not just for our financial predicament, but also for my father's health and well-being. From her deep experience in and knowledge of the health insurance industry, she was intimately familiar with our highly technical medical bills, the healthcare providers we were dealing with, and the tactics employed by my father's uncooperative travelers' insurer. She thoroughly explained her plan of action and what she expected to accomplish, and then immediately and relentlessly got to work on our behalf.

By the time Adria was done, she had saved us roughly $220,000, which represented a vast majority of my father's medical expenses! More importantly, while she was resolving bill after bill, she was giving my family the peace of mind to enjoy what remaining time we had with my father.

With healthcare costs skyrocketing and the health insurance industry becoming increasingly complicated, Adria is an asset to our communities. She has saved her clients in excess of $3,000,000 and received well-deserved accolades for her professional accomplishments, community leadership, and passion for service, ranging from the 2008 Insurance Professional of the Year Award (Insurance Professionals of Orange County, NY) to the 2011 Volunteer of the Year Award (Mental Health Association of Orange County) to being recognized as a "Woman of Achievement" in 2013 by New York's WCBS Newsradio 880. It gives me great pleasure to nominate Adria for *Westchester Magazine*'s Healthcare Hero award, and I sincerely hope that the Judging Committee will act favorably on this nomination.

Sharen and Brendan Kolnick

MedWise Insurance Advocacy, CEO, Adria Goldman Gross is a renowned figure in the Westchester area and across the country as a result of her extensive referral network of well-satisfied clients. Her clients are thrilled to refer friends and relatives in need of her unique talent as a Medical Claims Advocate, dealing with complex medical billing put forth by the interface of the health care delivery system and insurance marketplace.

The adversarial relationship between insurance payment and services billed in the course of the provision of medical services is all too often experienced by individuals within the nexus of a need to receive treatment and the equal need to have medical services reimbursed by insurance companies. The majority of people fall into the position of struggling to pay bills that have been denied by insurance companies.

One of Ms. Goldman Gross's clients wrote the following testimonial:

"If a medical insurance corporation is stone-walling your claim, don't argue with them---go see Adria Gross. Adria is not merely a top professional, she practically invented her profession. She is a passionate and empathic defender of the rights of her clients. She treats her clients like human beings and pays attention to their stories. She says that every case is different--I am sure that she devises a different strategy for every case. She certainly has a lot of strategies. She has spent years studying the system. She has a profound knowledge of the way medical insurance corporations work (or don't work) and she is familiar with both the legal and the financial aspects of each case.

We went to her because we were trying unsuccessfully to collect reimbursement for an emergency hospitalization that occurred in a foreign country. (It was clearly covered by our policy.) There was a lot of money at stake and there seemed to be no hope of ever seeing it again. But when Adria got to work, the stone wall began to crumble.

In the end, after months of stalling tactics, they finally ponied up the full amount. There's no way we could have recovered the money if Adria had not intervened. She moves mountains!"

Some people are blessed to have become aware of the services and rare ability of Ms. Goldman Gross to review technical contracts and rise to the challenge of dealing with insurance company bureaucrats in order to unravel the puzzle of reasoning as to exactly why the insurance company should in fact pay the bill rather than 'just denying" it. "Just denied" becomes "just approved" with the pleasant, reasonable interjection/discussion with Ms. Goldman Gross whose facile, logical intellect appears to make these unintelligible components come together for the client's benefit in what often appears as a heroic event.

Thrilled clients' reactions can only be described as the delight experienced by "Virginia" as she was told, "Yes, my dear, there is a Santa Claus," her name is Adria Goldman Gross, who in less than three years has saved over $3,000,000 for her clients.

Stacy Rittenberg

APPENDIX 3
Testimonials for MedWise and Adria Goldman Gross

"I cannot thank you enough for your recent medical bill advocacy on my behalf regarding an exorbitant medical bill for routine blood work. Feeling caught between a lab that was billing me and an insurance company that would not honor its claim, I turned to you for advocacy. You immediately allayed my concerns, worked closely with me, conducted valuable research and together we contacted the laboratory involved to resolve this issue, all within one week. Due to your stalwart involvement, the laboratory settled for a small payment-in-full that amounted to 24 times less than the lab originally charged for its work.

"You immediately brought to the lab's attention a fee amount that is usual, reasonable, customary and allowable, based on your expertise, and they immediately accepted the offer. It must also be stated that throughout this ordeal you remained accessible, personable, affable and good-humored, characteristics that certainly made me feel much better. It is clear to me that our system has been designed for profit on the part of insurance companies and others involved in the medical profession, as opposed to attending to the health of our citizenry. The system is also terribly complicated and bureaucratic. That said, it is good to know that there are decent individuals such as you, who can offer a helping hand at a time of need. I highly recommend your professional services without hesitation to anyone experiencing a medical billing issue. Together, we fought 'Goliath' and because of your advocacy, clearly 'David won the battle.'"

Robert Aloise

"I have known Adria for almost fifteen years. Over the years, Adria has [assisted] me and my family in many medical and health insurance matters. She has been able to create a resolution to every medical insurance difficulty that we have encountered . . . guiding us through the obstacles. Adria looks at the intricate details of the situation and is always able to solve whatever problems we face. Adria has demonstrated her ability to interpret all of our medical bill issues and decipher incorrect coding or human errors. With every distressed situation, Adria relieves our fears and trepidation. We feel blessed to know Adria and would recommend her to any organization or future ambition that she might desire."

R. Cloth

"Faced with the mounting paper work, and the run-around the insurance carrier was giving us, we were at a loss of where to turn. And then we found Adria, and MedWise. We are absolutely ecstatic that you were capable of reversing the multiple medical insurance denials. You took an amazing interest in not just the case, but a true and heartfelt interest in the ordeal that our daughter had gone through. It was as if you were working with your family. And for that alone we are truly grateful to you. Thank you for your responsive, professional and empathetic characteristics. We will unquestionably recommend your expertise to anyone that desires or needs a medical bill advocate."

Morty F.

"Adria is a very organized and detail-oriented woman who has a willingness to learn from the people she deals with. She works well under pressure and is quite capable in ensuring that the job gets done in a timely manner. Adria is a very committed, trustworthy and responsible business woman and always guards the confidential nature of her business dealings to protect everyone's privacy. Adria also is excellent at following through to get money for her clients from the insurance companies, developing relationships with key people who can move claims through the system. I would recommend Adria without any reservation to be a tremendous asset to every employer."

Susan S., LCSW

"Adria is definitely one of the most ethical and trustworthy persons I have ever encountered. With a willingness to go the extra mile . . . Adria demonstrates a generous spirit . . . standing up for the right thing when it comes to advocacy for others . . . . I would not hesitate to hire Adria in any capacity and recommend her most highly to your company."

Robin H.

"Due to MedWise Insurance Advocacy, within a short period of time my denied claim was paid. I experienced a test at a New York City hospital; all the bills were paid by my insurance carrier except for the pathology reports. The hospital is located in New York City and the pathology bills were sent from another state. The insurance company kept denying the claims since the bill was being sent from outside New York State. Adria Gross, at MedWise, realized the confusion and kept going up the ladder within the insurance company for them to understand, determine and agree that the claim was payable. Bravo to MedWise for contesting the claim to be paid! Thank you, Adria at MedWise, for your productive work and fortitude."

Jerris Mungai

"I've known Adria for several years and have had numerous opportunities to discuss business ideas and processes with her. I have gone to her numerous times for information and advice regarding her areas of expertise. Adria is extremely knowledgeable and always willing to help. She has received a great deal of recognition in her field, all of which is well deserved. I have no hesitation recommending Adria for all of your billing needs."

Laura Mann, Owner, Law Offices of Laura S. Mann, LLC

"I have known Adria Gross for over 20 years, and I am continually amazed by the depth and range of her remarkable intelligence, insightfulness, reliability, resourcefulness, limitless energy---and her ability to get the job done quickly, efficiently, and effectively. Adria remains a constant source of awe and inspiration with her capacity to think creatively about challenging problems and dilemmas, arriving at workable solutions in a very short time. Highly ethical, completely professional, and with an eye towards making a lasting difference in the world through her business practices, Adria brings new dimensions to the business relationship. It becomes a wonderful and memorable experience to participate in Adria's medical billing business and I encourage everyone to partake of her services. You won't be sorry."

Beth M., MSW, LCSW, BCD

"Adria . . . is an outstanding insurance advocate for many individuals and families. My family had a situation where our internal medicine physician did not have a contract with Medicare. For us to receive reimbursement from our secondary insurer, we were required to obtain a letter of denial from Medicare. We called on Adria and she was able to obtain a denial from Medicare and a reimbursement from our secondary insurer. Without Adria's assistance, I do not know if we could have ever received compensation for our medical bills. I would highly recommend Adria to all of my friends, colleagues, and clients as an effective communicator serving as a liaison between all patients, medical providers, attorneys and insurance companies with any medical insurance problems that surface."

G. Price, CPA

"Adria reviewed and analyzed medical bills and Medicare statements for us in a litigated matter and did a phenomenal job, enabling us to provide proof of the appropriateness of the amounts claimed. Adria is diligent and dedicated to her task, and I recommend her most highly. Top qualities: great results, personable, expert."

Steven Milligram

"I just wanted to thank you so very much for all the professional support, direction and recommendations you provided for me regarding my parents' health insurance issue. I am so appreciative that you were able to provide such a quick turnaround of information which enabled us to make very important decisions in a timely manner. I will surely be recommending you and your services where I can . . . you were a lifesaver and the support I so needed at such a difficult time."

    Kimberley B.

"Adria has the highest percentage of claims paid within thirty days. She quickly follows up on claims that were not paid and her follow-ups always led to quick resolutions. Adria always stays current with Medicare changes, insurance changes and regulations, as well as new CPT coding updates. Adria is professional, knowledgeable, ethical and highly motivated. She will be an asset in any work environment."

    Dr. B.

"Adria has provided excellent service for our company for many years. [She] has proven her expertise in billing issues, especially with Medicare. With our company, we deal with complicated, multi-code claim submissions. With Adria on these claims we do not have to worry about any denials . . . we are certain that we will receive payment. She gives her undivided attention to completing the process of submitting and payment of all claims. Adria is highly respected by our employees and us. She has had an amazing impact on our company's atmosphere. Adria always approaches her job as a professional businesswoman. We consider her a great asset to the company."

    O & P

"Adria Gross is a hard-working, conscientious professional. She is enthusiastic and keeps on top of the latest news and regulations in her industry. Her services would definitely add value to your company."

Karen Walker, Instructor, Orange County Community College

"I extend my sincerest thanks on behalf of my mother and my entire family for your hard work. I was overwhelmed with the sheer number of medical bills that continued to barrage me daily---that's when I turned to you. Your professionalism, sensitivity and timeliness helped to make a very difficult situation better. Your ability to negotiate with doctors and hospitals saved my mother both time and a great deal of money. Thank you for all you have done to help my family. I would recommend you and your company to anyone who needs help dealing with medical bills."

Catherine Redmond

"Adria helps me bring the best to my clients. She is extremely generous with her vast knowledge, and I call on her to answer tough medical billing questions for me and my clients. She knows the 'ins and outs' of the insurance industry and has the patience and persistence to get things done! Thank you, Adria! Top qualities: personable, expert, high integrity."

Karen Rosenberg Caccavo

"I just wanted to thank you for 'giving a hoot' and assisting me with questions I had regarding a medical billing issue. Although, in the end the answers that you provided were not quite the ones I wished to hear, I feel they were honest answers based on the information I provided. Honesty and integrity does matter. I hope to not ever be in this situation again, but if I do I will certainly remember to call upon MedWise Insurance Advocacy for a medical bill advocate. "

Kimberly Proctor

"I never imagined that I would ever see the compensation from the health insurance carrier. You continuously advised me to be positive, and you always believed you would be successful handling my case. Look at your accomplishment! The hospital bills were paid for by the insurance carrier after a semi-denial. You also assisted us in subrogating funds back from the hospital which we had previously paid . . . Thank you for your due diligence!! . . . I will recommend you to anyone with insurance problems. You are a remarkable outstanding patient advocate with a wealth of information. Thank you for persevering on behalf of your clients and certify they receive the monies they are entitled to."

Dr. John Mendola and Joan Mendola

"I strongly recommend Adria Gross of MedWise as someone you can rely on to assist your clients in determining what is right and wrong in both Medicare and private insurance claims against their judgments and/or settlements. From her experience as a claims processor in the insurance industry, she is familiar with the "games" that are played by insurers, as well as circumventing their tactics. Her familiarity with the diagnostic codes used by healthcare providers enabled her to highlight those claims she felt were inappropriate in my case to get to the legitimate ones."

N.D. Dunitz

"You are just AMAZING, a total angel... thank you, thank you, thank you!!!!

"I was recently saddled with almost $4000 in medical bills unexpectedly. What was incredibly frustrating is that I seemed unable to make any headway into solving the issue between the provider and my insurance company.

"I decided there must be such a thing as a medical advocate and immediately started an internet search to see if I could locate such a service. I found a few sites, but it was only Adria Gross's that made me feel comfortable about making the call. After scrolling through pages of solid testimonials on her site, I felt confident that if anyone could help me, it would be Adria!

"I was right! In less than 10 days, Adria had cut through all the levels of bureaucracy to find the exact right department to present the case. Not only did she present the case, but when the insurance company was unwilling to pay the claim, Adria argued the case and requested to go up even higher. Soon after that the case was settled, with the insurance company paying 100% of my bill.

"I should also mention that throughout the process, Adria stayed in constant contact with me via email and phone.

"Adria Gross is tops in my book, as well as in my pocket book! I have already referred her to a colleague and will continue to refer her, and her wonderful service, to everyone I know."

Elizabeth Khan

"I contacted Adria Gross of MedWise Billing in January 2014. During this time I had been without health insurance and had just received treatment at a local medical group for a routine Colles fracture of the wrist. Upon receipt of my final medical bills for 2 doctors visits and 2 x-rays I was astounded at the cost and realized that I had been billed way and above the ordinary and customary charges that a patient with insurance would have been required to pay. Adria Gross was immediately responsive to my pleas for help. She was well connected with people in high places and well informed as to how to dismantle the brick wall of my medical group's billing agency. Moreover she was willing to go the extra mile for my case and charge me a very reasonable amount for her services after the negotiations were successful.

"I am very pleased to recommend Adria Gross and MedWise Billing to anyone who has been victimized by our current medical billing system and doesn't have an insurance company to dispute unfair charges. She cares about the man on the street and is a powerful resource against corruption in medicine."

Sincerely,
Sarah Mace

"Last year, my daughter was hospitalized with a mental breakdown in the psychiatric ward for about ten days, and then was treated as an outpatient at the hospital for a period following.

"On the traumatic Thursday that I placed her on an involuntary hold at the hospital, I realized that she would turn 24 years old on the upcoming Sunday, and her insurance as a family member under my insurance plan would end. So I had to scramble all day that Friday to get the insurance company to confirm that she would be covered under a pre-existing condition for her hospital stay. At the end of the day I had barely managed to be successful, and knew that my daughter could stay in the hospital without major financial damage.

"After my daughter was discharged from the hospital, the hospital bill came, and it was $12,530.16 over what my insurance was willing to pay. After several months of trying to negotiate the bill by myself, I was discouraged and getting nowhere. Eventually, I was desperately facing a threat by the hospital to go to collections.

"I now know just how stressful it is to be worried sick about a family member, and providing care, holding down a job, while at the same time, having to deal with the confusing and byzantine world of health insurance coverage.

"A friend of mine recommended that I try to find a 'health care consultant.'

"I didn't even know that there were such people. After a search, I found Adria at MedWise.

"Adria, quite simply, came to my rescue. She was warm and friendly and caring, and immediately put my mind at ease by explaining what she would be able to do. Adria was available any time I needed to get in touch with her.

"I sent her all my notes and paperwork, and she immediately got to work on my behalf. The stress of dealing with the bills was taken off my plate, and I immediately felt better.

"Not only did Adria help with my daughter's hospital bill, she was also able to reduce or have dismissed several other doctor and therapy bills that insurance was refusing to cover.

"Adria has a stellar knowledge of the health insurance industry, and she gets results. At the end of her work on my behalf, she was able to save me a total of $13,370! It was well worth the reasonable rates she charged. I could never have been able to get the same results on my own.

"I wish that everyone knew about Adria and her work. I can't recommend Adria highly enough. It is exceedingly difficult to be an advocate for yourself in health insurance billing, and Adria's expert advice is invaluable."

Connie R.

"If you are faced with the byzantine world of medical bills, contact Adria NOW. She not only saved us thousands of dollars in medical expenses, she gave us that most wonderful of gifts: peace of mind. Her fees are amazingly reasonable, and she is also a delight to work with. She will work ferociously on your behalf with insurance companies, hospitals and doctors. I will never deal with another large medical expense again without hiring Adria first! Thanks for all you do!!"

Sarah

"To Whom It May Concern,

As I was seeking assistance with care regarding insurance issues and medical cost negotiations, if this were to become necessary, I turned to the internet. I found MedWise Insurance Advocacy, Inc., and I was immediately impressed. It was everything I was looking for when I started my search. I called the number immediately and Adria Gross, the owner, answered her phone and listened to the problems I had been encountering with the insurance company and phone calls due to claims not being paid. She was very empathetic and immediately took a valued interest in the issues shared. I knew that minute I would hire her to assist with my insurance issues.

"I sent the necessary information to help Adria's company to assist me with my bills, and insurance information. Once the information sent was reviewed, I received a phone call from Adria which lasted four hours. Together we called all of the relevant hospitals, clinics, and various small physician groups. We then called the insurance company and found the information sent to them had been enough to reverse their denial of coverage due to a pre-existing clause, and the claims will be paid as of February 1, 2014. After hearing the information, I was still unclear to the meaning shared by the customer service representative. Having Adria on the phone with me to explain the information was invaluable.

"Adria has been a godsend to me as I have attempted to traverse through the difficult challenges of the insurance company and medical facilities requiring payment. It is obvious Adria truly has a heart for those families and individuals who are denied coverage and then get the run-around from insurance companies. She also has the gracious spirit to help others. I have the utmost confidence in and admiration for Adria. In this day and time it is rare to find one who is more dedicated and motivated toward serving others.

Claudia S.

"We received a medical bill for over $3,000 for an MRI that should have been covered by insurance. Insurance denied the claim, and we ran into multiple roadblocks with both the provider and the insurance company. Adria Gross with MedWise was able to walk us through the appeal process and help guide us through the otherwise confusing insurance process. What a relief it was to get a letter from the insurance company stating that the appeal had been approved and they would pay our claim in full! I would highly recommend Adria for anyone needing assistance dealing with health insurance claims. Great service and very responsive. Thanks, Adria."

B. Ray

"If a medical insurance corporation is stone-walling your claim, don't argue with them-- go see Adria Gross. Adria is not merely a top professional, she practically invented her profession. She is a passionate and empathic defender of the rights of her clients. She treats her clients like human beings and pays attention to their stories. She says that every case is different--I am sure that she devises a different strategy for every case. She certainly has a lot of strategies. She has spent years studying the system. She has a profound knowledge of the way medical insurance corporations work (or don't work) and she is familiar with both the legal and the financial aspects of each case. She stays on top of current developments.

"We went to her because we were trying unsuccessfully to collect reimbursement for an emergency hospitalization that occurred in a foreign country. (It was clearly covered by our policy.) There was a lot of money at stake and there seemed to be no hope of ever seeing it again. But when Adria got to work, the stone wall began to crumble. In the end, after months of stalling tactics, they finally ponied up the full amount. There's no way we could have recovered the money if Adria had not intervened. She moves mountains!"

Naomi Rosenblau and Mick Stern

"Surgery is terrifying enough; the endless insurance hassles waiting on the other side are mind-boggling. After a year of making every effort to resolve an exorbitant and unreasonable surgical fee, I was fortunate enough to find Adria Gross. She was the first person who was able to make sense of the system for me. In addition to resolving my billing problems, she shared my outrage at the unfair bills that were arriving on my doorstep. For the first time in a year, I felt like I had someone on my side. Adria is knowledgeable and caring, and I can't recommend her highly enough. Thanks again!"

Kate

"If you are looking for a medical insurance advocate, I can highly recommend Ms. Gross. She is a force of nature! She reviewed all of our information rapidly and was able to cut to the heart of it all in two sentences. Adria reduced our bill from $6,300 to $190 within a couple days. She was very direct and professional in her communications with us and everyone she contacted on our behalf."

Mel Hughes

"In one 30-minute phone consultation, Adria was able to help me settle an issue I had been battling for 5 months and was able to reduce my bill by $1,100. Thanks, Adria!!"

Kaity R.

"My name is Bianey Paramo and I would just like to take the time to say how thankful my family and I are to Adria Gross for helping us resolve a very big hospital bill, above $23,000. I have four children and my husband is the only one who works, and it worried us on how we were going to pay the amount. I thank God for meeting Adria Gross and all of her hard work in turning $23,000 to just $600. I hope

God sends her many blessings and helps her to keep helping people that are in the same situation we were in, because without her we wouldn't have solved this problem."

Bianey Paramo